Framework Poetry

Journeys

Poetry and Literacy at 11–14

Wendy Bardsley

(a former Advisory Teacher with the Manchester Education
Authority and published poet)

Laura Sanderson

(English teacher at Boston Spa Comprehensive)

Published by HarperCollinsPublishers Limited
77-85 Fulham Palace Rd
Hammersmith
London
W6 8JB

www.CollinsEducation.com
http://www.CollinsEducation.com
On-line support for schools and colleges

©HarperCollinsPublishers 2002

ISBN 000 711 388 9

10 9 8 7 6 5 4 3 2

Wendy Bardsley and Laura Sanderson assert their moral rights to be identified as the authors of this work.

British Library Cataloguing in Publication Data

A catalogue record for this publication is available from the British Library.

ACKNOWLEDGEMENTS

TEXT: 'Making a Poem' from Collected Poems by Edwin Morgan and reprinted by permission of Carcanet Press Limited, 1985, p13; 'The Seal' from The Mermaid's Purse by Ted Hughes and reprinted by permission of Faber and Faber Limited, 1999, p15; 'Mother Sea Lion' taken from Collected Poems by Les Murray and reprinted by permission of Carcanet Press Limited, 1998, p17; 'A Small Dragon' by ©Brian Patten, reprinted by permission of Penguin Books Ltd, p21; 'The Thought Fox' from The Hawk in the Rain by Ted Hughes, reprinted by permission of Faber and Faber Limited, p25; 'Friends' taken from The Secret Brother by Elizabeth Jennings and reprinted by permission of Macmillan Publishers Ltd, 2000, p27; 'A Pen Friend' from The Myth of the Twin by John Burnside. Published by Jonathan Cape and reprinted by kind permission of The Random House Group Ltd, p29; 'Astronauts' is reproduced courtesy of Tim Kendall, p33; 'Do you ever think we'll get to see Earth, Sir?' from Selected Poems by Sheenagh Pugh and reprinted by permission of Seren, 1990, p34; 'The Morning Moon' from Collected Poems by Derek Walcott and reprinted by permission of Faber and Faber Limited, 1992, p36; 'Wolf Man' from Steel Wings by Wendy Bardsley and reprinted by permission of Headland Publications, 1998, p39; 'Worm' from Householder by Gerard Woodward. Published by Chatto & Windus and reprinted by permission of the Random House Group Ltd, p41; 'The Earthquake' from Lines from a Legend © Bibhu Padhi, p43; 'Early Autumn' from Dante's Drum-Kit by Douglas Dunn, reprinted by permission of Faber and Faber Limited, 1993, p48; 'Autumn Verses' from BBC's Favourite Poems by John Hegley, reprinted by permission of Methuen Publishing Limited, p51; 'Serenades' by Seamus Heaney from Collected Poems reprinted by permission of Faber and Faber Limited, p54; 'Eagle in New Mexico' by D. H. Lawrence from The Complete Poems of D. H. Lawrence, reprinted by kind permission of Laurence Pollinger Limited and the Estate of Frieda Lawrence Ravagli, p58; 'The Eagle' from Cacti by Matthew Sweeney, reprinted by permission of Secker and Warburg Publishers, 1992, p60; 'The Highwayman' by Alfred Noyes, reprinted by kind permission of The Society of Authors as the literary representative of the Estate of Alfred Noyes, p62; 'Tropical Death' from The Fat Black Woman by Grace Nichols reprinted by permission of Little, Brown and Company (UK), p71; 'Survivor' by Roger McGough, reprinted by permission of PFD on behalf of ©Roger McGough, p72; 'In the Attic' from The Pleasure Steamers by Andrew Motion reprinted by permission of Carcanet Press Limited, p77; 'Dad' from Selected Poems by Elaine Feinstein, reprinted by permission of Carcanet Press Limited, p78; 'East Moors' from Collected Poems by Gillian Clarke, reprinted by permission of Carcanet Press Limited, p80; 'Away and See' from Mean Time by Carol Anne Duffy, reprinted by permission of Anvil Press Poetry in 1993, p82; 'Before You Cut Loose' from The Dead Sea Poems by Simon Armitage, reprinted by permission of Faber and Faber Limited, p86; 'Nature and free Animals' from Selected Poems by Stevie Smith, reprinted by permission of Penguin Books Ltd., on behalf of the estate of James MacGibbon, p88; 'The Captured Tiger' is reproduced with permission of Hazel Streeter, p92; 'Chippenham' by Fleur Adcock from Poems 1960-2000, published by Bloodaxe Books, 2000, p98; 'Dead Thick' from Storm Damage ©Brian Patten, 1988, first published by Unwin Paperback in 1988. Permission given by Brian Patten care of Rogers, Coleridge and White, p101; 'I Luv Me Mudder' ©Benjamin Zephaniah, p103; 'The Telling Part' by Jakie Kay from The Adoption Papers, published by Bloodaxe Books, 1991, p105; 'Memres of Alfred Stoker' from The Echoey Tunnel by Christopher Reid, reprinted by permission of Faber and Faber Limited, p107; 'Dulce Et Decorum Est' by Wilfred Owen, reprinted by permission of The Random House Group, p110; 'The Dornier' from The Glass Island by Gladys Mary Coles, reprinted by permission of Duckworth, 1992 and 1994, p112; 'Started Orders' from Birthmarks by Mick Imlah, published by Chatto & Windus. Reprinted by permission of The Random House Group Ltd, p114.

THUMBNAILS OF POETS: Libraries: Hulton Getty :William Blake: John Clare, Christina Rossetti, Alfred Noyes, Dylan Thomas, Alfred, Lord Tennyson, Percy Bysshe Shelley, D.H. Lawrence, William Wordsworth. Mary Evans Picture Library: Emily Dickinson, Emily Brontë, W.B. Yeats, William Shakespeare. Carcanet Press: Gillian Clarke, Elaine Feinstein, Edwin Morgan, Elizabeth Jennings, Les Murray. The National Portrait Gallery: Wilfred Owen, Benjamin Zephaniah. The Brontë Museum: Patrick Brontë.

All other thumbnails have been supplied by the respective publishers or poets themselves: Douglas Dunn © Fay Godwin; Brian Patten © Richard Braine (Penguin); Roger McGough (Puffin Books); Gladys Mary Coles © Joe Edwards; Jackie Kay © Ingrid Pollard; Carol Anne Duffy © Sue Adler; Grace Nichols © Sheila Geraghty; Sheenagh Pugh © Bernard Mitchell; John Hegley © John Sleeman; Derek Walcott and Christopher Reid © Nigel Parry; Simon Armitage © Jason Bell; Andrew Motion © Antonio Olmos; Seamus Heaney and Ted Hughes © Caroline Forbes; Mick Imlah © Julian Bond; Wendy Bardsley © Mike Frisby;

MAIN ILLUSTRATIONS: p10: Corbis Images; p11: Bridgeman Art Library; p12-13: Corbis Images; p15: FitzWilliam Museum, Cambridge; p15: Bridgeman Art Library; p17: Stone; p20, 21 and 24: Bridgeman Art Library; p25 Stone; p31: Bridgeman Art Library; p 32: Corbis Images; p34, 37 and 39: Stone; p43-4: PA Photos; p 45: Stone; p47: Bridgeman Art Library; p48: Corbis Images; p50-51: Corbis Images; p54: Stone; p57: Corbis Images; p58 Stone; p60: Corbis Images; p64: OUP (illustration by Charles Keeping); p67: The Ronald Grant Archive; p68: Stone; p71: The Bridgeman Art Library; p77: Stone; p79: Life File; p80: The Photo Library: Wales; p83 Life File; p87 Artville; p89: artwork by Chandra at NB Illustration; p91: Stone; p93: National Geographic; p95 and 97: Stone; p99: artwork by Chandra at NB illustration; p106: artwork by Louise Hilton at NB Illustration; p108, 111 and 113: Hulton Getty;

DESIGN BY Blue Pig Design

COVER IMAGE COURTESY OF Stone

COMMISSIONING EDITOR Helen Clark

PROJECT MANAGEMENT BY Charlie Evans

EDITED BY Charlie Evans and Nancy Terry

PERMISSIONS CLEARED BY Gavin Jones

Journeys Literacy Framework Matching Grid

	Unit	Word Level	Sentence Level	Text Level Reading	Text Level Writing	Speaking and Listening
All Years	What is a Poem?	15, 21		2, 4, 8, 12, 14, 19	1, 2, 3, 8, 11	1, 5, 7, 13
Year 7	Creatures of the Sea & Shore	15, 21		2, 4, 5, 7, 8, 9, 12, 14	2, 3, 19, 11	2, 1, 13, 7, 5
Year 7	Mythical Beasts	15, 16	15	12, 14, 6	2, 8, 4, 11	3, 13
Year 7	Foxes	10		19, 2, 4, 8, 14, 12	2, 14, 19, 11	12, 13
Year 7	Friendship & Loyalty	15		7, 19, 2, 4	1, 3, 14, 11	13, 7, 12
Year 7	Space	16, 15		2, 4, 7, 8, 12, 14	11	12, 13, 7, 1, 5
Year 7	Moon	15, 21	15	4, 14, 12	2	12, 13, 7, 3
Year 8	Earth	7c, 11, 9		5, 10, 11	3, 9. 17	10
Year 8	Autumn	11, 9, 7c, 14	13	5, 7, 11	3	10
Year 8	Birdsong	7b, 14, 11	12	3, 5, 11, 10	3, 17, 7, 9	10
Year 8	Eagles	9, 7c, 11		11, 5, 10, 2	3, 17	10, 3
Year 8	Love	9, 11		14, 5, 10, 11, 2	1, 3, 17, 2	10
Year 8	Loss	9, 11		5, 7, 10, 11, 14	3, 9, 17	10, 5
Year 9	Remembering	7	4	6, 7, 11, 9	17, 2	
Year 9	Words to a Loved One	7	4	3, 7, 9	2,	
Year 9	Guilt	7	4, 9	9	2, 17	
Year 9	Freedom	7	4	7, 3, 9	8, 2	
Year 9 & Pre-GCSE	Learning	7	4, 11	3, 6, 6	2, 17	8, 10
Year 9 & Pre-GCSE	Mothers	7	10, 4	7, 6, 3	2, 17	
Year 9 & Pre-GCSE	War	7	4	7, 6, 3	17, 2	

Journeys Contents Grid

		Title	Poet
Unit 12	Love	The Highwayman	Alfred Noyes
		Sonnet 17*	William Shakespeare
Unit 13	Loss	Do Not Go Gentle Into That Good Night	Dylan Thomas
		Tropical Death	Grace Nichols
		Survivor	Roger McGough
		I Felt a Funeral in My Brain*	Emily Dickinson
Unit 14	Remembering	When You Are Old*	W. B. Yeats
		In The Attic	Andrew Motion
		Dad	Elaine Feinstein
		East Moors	Gillian Clarke
Unit 15	Words to a Loved One	Away and See	Carol Anne Duffy
		A Dirge*	Christina Rossetti
Unit 16	Guilt	Before You Cut Loose	Simon Armitage
		Nature and Free Animals	Stevie Smith
Unit 17	Freedom	The Tiger*	William Blake
		The Captured Tiger	Hazel Streeter
Unit 18	Learning	The Tables Turned*	William Wordsworth
		Chippenham	Fleur Adcock
		Dead Thick	Brian Patten
Unit 19	Mothers	I Love Me Mudder	Benjamin Zephaniah
		The Telling Part	Jackie Kay
		From: Memres of Alfred Stoker	Chistopher Reid
Unit 20	War	Dulce et Decorum Est*	Wilfred Owen
		The Dornier (A Farmer's Story)	Gladys Mary Coles
		Starter's Orders	Mick Imlah

Year 8

Year 9

Pre-GCSE

* indicates pre-1914

Introduction

Journeys is an exciting new collection of poetry for schools containing both a wealth of classic poems from the national literary heritage, and some remarkable contemporary work.

The book has been specifically compiled to fulfil the requirements of the English Framework for years 7, 8 and 9 with lesson activities that address Framework objectives. Background information is provided for the poems as well as a factfile on each poet. Technical terms have been highlighted and explained.

The wide range of poetry contained in the book means that each unit can be simply dipped into or followed through over several lessons. Each unit has been structured in order to give a sense of progression.

- The Starter activity is intended as a quick exercise to get pupils thinking about the themes they will encounter in the poetry.

- The Introduction exercises are to help pupils examine the main features of the poems.

- The Development exercises are designed for closer investigation of the language, themes and poetic techniques.

- The Plenaries can be used to quickly summarise and consolidate what has been covered.

The contemporary poetry (some of which may be new to the classroom) has been chosen where natural and genuine links could be found to pre-1914 classics. The Development exercises often require pupils to compare the diverse ways in which different poets have approached a similar theme, helping to explore the ways in which language evolves over time, as well as the historical and cultural context of the classics. This provides a rich and enjoyable perspective in which to understand poetry and its overall relationship with feeling and language in general.

 Writing   Discussion   Reading    Class activity   Pair work   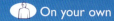 On your own

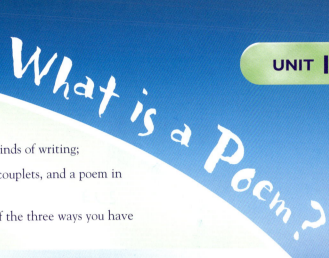

What is a Poem?

AIMS

- Look at some of the thoughts that poets have had about poetry;

- See how poetry differs from other kinds of writing;

- Study a haiku, a poem in rhyming couplets, and a poem in free verse;

- Write a poem of your own in any of the three ways you have learned about.

1 Starter

 Below are some ideas that poets have had about poetry. Read them carefully and think about them. In groups, bearing in mind the quotations below, discuss why people might choose to write poetry rather than prose.

Ted Hughes

What matters most, since we are listening to poetry and not to prose, is that we hear the song and dance in the words.

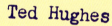

Elaine Feinstein

Poetry is language infused with the sharpest intensity of experience. More fiercely and more intimately than in prose, we recognise our own ordinary lives. That is why memorable lines of a great poet hold a particular power to strengthen the human spirit.

Seamus Heaney

Poetry is something essential to you, something you recognise instinctively as a true-sounding aspect of yourself and your own experience.

William Wordsworth

Poetry is the spontaneous overflow of powerful feelings.

Wendy Bardsley

Poetry is the art of composing, in condensed language, the rhythms, intensities and associated ideas of deeply felt emotional states.

Gillian Clarke

You can do anything with images. A poet can make anything, do anything, make us see, hear, feel, smell, taste, imagine anything she wants.

Michael Rosen

People disagree about very important things. Things like money, sex, race, bombs, school, parents, work... We must also agree with each other but we won't unless we discuss or argue it out. Poems are ways of beginning such arguments.

As you can see, there are many ways of thinking about poetry. As you go through the units, you will find out more about how a poem is made and begin to shape your own ideas.

Looking at Form

Every poem has a kind of **form**. The form is the shape that a poem lives in. As a class, talk about the kinds of poems you know about already.

Copy out the diagram below. Tick any of the forms you know that are listed. Discuss what you have recorded with a partner and explain what you understand by the ones you have selected.

Form	Tick if you don't know the word	Tick if you think you know the word	If you know the word, write a brief definition.
Kenning			
Limerick			
Riddle			
Cinquain			
Tanka			
Nonsense verse			
Sonnet			

Below are three forms you are going to look at in this unit:

- haiku;
- rhyming couplet;
- free verse.

Haiku: a form of Japanese poetry which has three lines.

The first line has 5 syllables.

The second has 7 syllables.

The third has 5 syllables.

This makes 17 syllables altogether.

> A **syllable** is a sound on its own. Water, for instance is a two-syllable word: wa/ter. Sometimes people try to write other forms of haiku, but the three-line version of 5, 7, 5 is the authentic Japanese version.

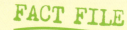

FACT FILE

William Mundy studies at Manchester Grammar School and is 16 years old. He wrote his haiku, he says, "Because I wanted to see how descriptive an image I could write using a limited structure."

A haiku is a short poem that makes you concentrate on a single idea. You can write a haiku on any subject you like.

The Globe
(Microcosm)

Looking at a globe
Every country is in place,
But where are the clouds?

William Mundy

2 Introduction

Discuss the following questions and be prepared to feed back your answers to the class.

- Look up the word 'Microcosm' in a dictionary. Does it help you understand what the haiku is about?

- Globes obviously don't show clouds, but can you think of any other things that might not be represented on them?

- What is the effect of the shortness of the haiku?

- What can you say about the language used?

- What is the single idea on which the haiku has been focused?

3 Development

Try to write a haiku of your own. Remember – it can be on any topic you choose.

You may want to use one of the following ideas: winter, holidays, school, my pet.

Begin by brainstorming all the ideas that occur to you when you think of the subject. Once you have lots of ideas down, then focus on one main thought or one of the five senses and try to fit your words to the haiku framework.

The second poem is 'Infant Sorrow' by William Blake.

FACT FILE

William Blake was born in London in 1757. At the age of 14 he became an apprentice engraver and later, when he was 21, he was accepted at the new Royal Academy at Somerset House. In 1783 his first poems were printed. His great talents as a painter and poet developed rapidly and he published many poems and paintings which have now become famous in our literary heritage. His poems range from the beautifully simple to the immense and mysterious. William Blake died in 1827.

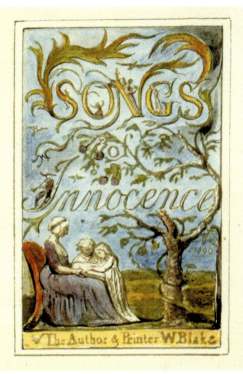

Infant Sorrow

My mother groaned, my father wept!
Into the dangerous world I leapt,
Helpless, naked, piping loud,
Like a fiend hid in a cloud.

Struggling in my father's hands,
Striving against my swaddling bands,
Bound and weary, I thought best
To sulk upon my mother's breast.

William Blake

'Infant Sorrow' is written in two four-line stanzas of rhyming couplets. **Rhyming couplets** are two lines that follow each other which rhyme together.

A **stanza** is a group of two or more lines in a poem, arranged in a pattern to form a section of a poem. It is like a paragraph in prose, but the lines are in verse.

Rhythm (in poetry) is where the words are arranged into patterns of sound. These patterns are created by the stresses of the syllables in the words.

1 Introduction

Choose someone in your group to read the poem out loud. How many beats per line are there? Think about the rhymes you can hear in the reading. You may need to listen again.

Quickly note all the rhymes you hear in the poem. Bracket together the words that rhyme with each other.

Look at how the groups of lines are arranged in the poem. What do you notice about them?

Quickly write two sentences using the words 'rhyming couplets' and 'stanza' to describe 'Infant Sorrow'.

Prepare two readings of 'Infant Sorrow'; one with a quick cheerful rhythm and one with a slow sad rhythm.

Discuss the two readings. Which rhythm reflected the meaning of the poem best?

2 Development

Answer the following questions in complete sentences.

- How many lines does each stanza in 'Infant Sorrow' have?
- How many rhyming couplets are there in each stanza?
- How many beats are there in each line of the poem?
- How does the rhythm help to reflect the poem's meaning?

Using the notes you have made during the lesson, and bringing in the words 'stanza', 'rhyming' and 'rhythm', write a paragraph about the way Blake has formed his poem.

The **theme** of a poem is what it is mainly about. Here, though, Blake is saying this poem may be about birth, but that it is a sorrowful affair. This is his point of view.

In writing, explain why Blake is suggesting that birth is a sad matter. Use the following paragraph openers to help you write about the poem.

- The world that the child leaps into is…
- The line which suggests the poet's parents are not very happy is…
- The words, 'Like a fiend hid in a cloud', suggest the poet is thinking…
- Other words that suggest the child didn't want to be born are…

Find the words: 'swaddling', 'bound' and 'sulk' in a dictionary, then answer the following questions in writing:

- What do you think is meant by the line, 'Striving against my swaddling band.'?
- What sort of image do you have when you read that the child is 'Bound and weary'?
- Why might the baby sulk?

Copy the star diagram below into your book. Scan the lines of Blake's poem for words that express his particular point of view or opinion about birth.

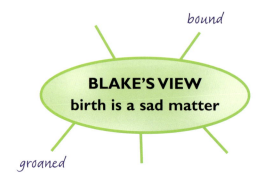

BLAKE'S VIEW
birth is a sad matter

bound

groaned

FACT FILE

Edwin Morgan was born in Glasgow in 1920. Till 1980 he taught in the English department at Glasgow University and became emeritus professor. His work is often highly original and experimental. Comedy plays an important part in his poetic imagination, as do ingenious wordplay and formal verse. He has won the Queen's Gold Medal for his contribution to poetry.

The third poem, by Edwin Morgan, is in **free verse**. Free verse leaves the poet free to write just as he likes in a form that comes naturally. A free-verse poem is driven by the **rhythm** of the words. Rhythm is the pattern of sounds that come from the syllables.

1 Introduction

This free-verse poem flows from Morgan's mind as he writes it. This is called writing in a **stream of consciousness**. Morgan is describing how the poet comes in from the cold with the words of the poem going round in his head. He then tries to write it. In this poem, he lets us in on what it is like to write a poem and some of the problems trying to hold on to the words.

Scan the lines to see how he tells us of the things that threaten to break his concentration. What are they?

2 Development

In groups, look at the following questions and make notes on your answers. Add any other interesting ideas that may come up. Be prepared to feedback your answers to the class.

- What is the poem about?
- What does Edwin Morgan mean when he says your poem must be prepared 'with luck'?
- How do the words 'dreaming a minute lightly' fit in with writing a poem?
- What do you understand by Morgan's suggestion that you should agree with your poem, and love it?
- If a poem becomes 'too fierce for favour', what does Edwin Morgan say you should do?
- Can you think of two reasons why Edwin Morgan might have decided to write this poem in free verse?

Making a Poem

Coming in with it
from frost and buses
gently burning
you must prepare it
with luck
to go critical.
Give the hook your scarf,
the chrome hook, maybe,
your green scarf. Say
Smoky Smoky
to the cat, set him
on his cushion, perhaps
a patch cushion
from old Perth.
Put the kettle on,
go to the window,
mist the glass
dreaming a minute lightly,

boys on the ice,
rows of orange lamps.
And go cut
white new bread.
Make tea like skaters' leaves.
You're never free.
It's blue dark night again.
Below the panes
in quietness.
Take a pencil
like the milkman's horse
round and round.
But you must agree
with it, and love it,
even when it grows
too fierce for favour.
It comes, and the cat shines.
And makes the poem now.

Edwin Morgan

3 Plenary

What have you learned about poetry that you did not know before?

Did sharing your work with somebody else help you? In what way?

If reading Edwin Morgan's poem has made you more confident about writing a poem, how has this happened?

Give the names of the three poetic forms about which you have have been learning.

See if you can add one more idea to 'What is a Poem?' at the start of the unit.

4 Homework

Choose one of the forms you have studied and try to write a poem of your own on anything that interests you. Bring your poem to the next session to discuss with a partner.

Go through the notes you have made on 'What is a Poem?', and think about them. Exchange poems with a friend and comment on each other's work, bearing in mind the following points:

- Have you used interesting language?
- If you rhymed your lines, did you do it cleverly?
- Is what you are saying easily understood?

You might now need to make changes, or improvements, to your poem. The first writing of it is called a **draft**. When you correct it and write it again, this is called **redrafting**. Look at the scribbles on the poem to the right. This is the poem 'Ode to the Nightingale' by the famous poet, John Keats, who wrote many beautiful Odes. Notice how he did not get it right first time!

Writing your poem and redrafting it is called the **process**. The process is just as important as the **product**, which is your finished work.

AIMS

- To compare two poems about sea creatures written by poets from two different cultures;
- To understand what is meant by personification;
- To use a thesaurus and dictionary;
- To skim for meaning;
- To reread for fuller understanding;
- To create diagrams to expand on meaning;
- To learn about assonance in poetry.

1 Starter

With a partner, talk about creatures you have found on the seashore and what they were like. Did they seem lost, tired, afraid, or something else? What did you do when you discovered them? Write a list of adjectives to describe the creatures. Be prepared to read these back to the class.

or

In groups, research seals and sea lions in the library or on the internet. Find out as many facts as you can about their habitat and how they live. Be prepared to give a presentation to the class on what you find.

In this first poem, 'Seal', Ted Hughes uses language that gives a vivid and memorable image of a baby seal.

Seal

Where Ocean heaved
A breast of silk
And a black jag reef
Boiled into milk

There bobbed up a head
With eyes as wild
And wide and dark
As a famine child.

I thought, by the way
It stared at me,
It had lost its mother
In the sea.

Ted Hughes

FACT FILE

Ted Hughes was born in 1930 in Mytholmroyd, Yorkshire and died in 1998 in Devon. He married the poet Sylvia Plath in 1956 and taught creative writing at Amherst College. Ted Hughes published many collections of poetry and is often viewed as a Nature poet. He became Poet Laureate in 1984.

2 Introduction

Skim the poem and pick out words that best describe the ocean. Skimming a poem means searching quickly for special information. Copy the star diagram below to organise your findings.

The Ocean

heaved

Now do the same thing for the seal. Again, one of the answers has been added.

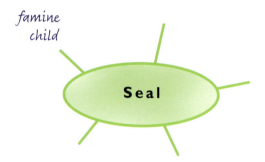

famine child

Seal

Compare your work with someone else's. Do the words you have found help to deepen your understanding of the poem? Ask your teacher to show you how to use a thesaurus to find some other words that are similar. Words like this are known as **synonyms**. Add the words to your diagrams.

3 Development

In your groups, discuss the questions below. Be prepared to feed your answers back to the class.

> *In his poem, Hughes says the eyes of the seal were 'wild/And wide and dark/As a famine child'. Comparing one thing with another like this by saying 'as' or 'like' is called using a* **simile**.

What does this comparison say about how the poet is thinking about the seal? Why is this simile effective? (Remember to use a dictionary for words that are difficult, and be prepared to feedback your ideas to the class.)

> *The long sound of 'i' in the words 'wild', 'wide' and 'child', are known as* **assonance**. *Notice how these sounds lend power to the poem. Assonance occurs when the same vowel sound is repeated in a line of poetry.*

The atmosphere of the poem is the 'mood' it is in. What sort of mood, or atmosphere, does Hughes create in the poem? Is it happy or is it sad? Or might it be something else?

FACT FILE

Les Murray was born in Nabiac, on the north coast of New South Wales in Australia, and grew up on his father's dairy farm. He is a prolific writer of prose and poetry, and has strong views on many subjects – war and violence in particular. Les Murray also writes poetry on themes of landscape, family, farm and animals. The second poem, 'Mother Sea Lion', is an example of this.

Mother Sea Lion

My pup has become myself
yet I'm still present.

My breasts have vanished.
My pup has grown them on herself.

Tenderly we rub whiskers.
She, me, both still present.

I plunge, dive deep in the Clench.
My blood erects. Familiar joy.

Coming out, I swim the beach-shingle.
Blood subsides. Yet I enjoy still.

Les Murray

Introduction

In Hughes' poem, the poet is talking about the baby seal, whereas Les Murray talks as if he himself is the mother sea lion. When a poet makes an idea or thing into a 'person', it is known as **personification**.

  Discuss the following questions in groups and make notes. Be prepared to share your ideas with the class.

- The mother sea lion says, 'My pup has become myself/yet I'm still present'. What does this mean?
- How might the mother sea lion rubbing whiskers with her baby assure her that they are 'both still present'?
- What do you understand by 'the Clench'?
- Murray says the mother sea lion 'swims' the beach-shingle. How might she enjoy her life on the seashore as well as her life in the sea?
- How does calling the sea 'a breast of silk' make it seem?
- Can you pick out the words that show that the mother sea lion is already thinking of her baby as independent?
- How does the mother sea lion feel about her pup?

Development

The word **atmosphere** is used to describe the mood of a piece of writing. What can you say about the atmosphere in each poem? How is the situation of the baby seal in the first poem different from that of the baby sea lion in the second? Copy the following chart into your book and read the poems again to help you with your answers.

Both poets write about a sea creature, though in a different way. Which of the poems is easiest to understand? Discuss your choice with your partner. Write a paragraph explaining why you have chosen this poem.

	Seal	Mother Sea Lion
Atmosphere in the poem		
The way the sea is described		
Safety of the baby in the poem		

Plenary

Think about your aims at the start of the unit, and answer the following:

- Pick out some words that have been combined for poetic effect. For example: 'eyes as wild'.
- How would you skim for meaning? In what way is skimming a poem different from reading it carefully?
- Explain the difference between a synonym and a simile.
- Say what you understand by personification.
- What does it mean when assonance is used in a poem?

Homework

Using the notes you have made so far, write a paragraph comparing the two poems. Make sure you include the following points:

- The situation the baby seal appears to be in as well as that of the baby sea lion.
- The points of view from which the poems are written – who is speaking in each poem.
- Which of the poems you enjoyed particularly and why.

Mythical Beasts

AIMS

- To develop skills in finding the meaning of words from their context in a poem;
- To use a dictionary to confirm and clarify meaning;
- To look carefully at language used before 1914;
- To give a briefly rehearsed talk and answer questions pertinently;
- To think about the importance of myths in the world of writing and imagination.

1 Starter

Myths are simply tales about supernatural people or things, and yet they are part of our collective imagination and constantly expand and colour the work of writers. We are all intrigued by the thought of a mythical beast. The following poems by Alfred, Lord Tennyson and Brian Patten are both about such creatures.

Spend five minutes making a list of as many mythical beasts as you can think of from films, books or other sources. How many types can you identify as a class?

FACT FILE

Alfred, Lord Tennyson was born in 1809 and became Poet Laureate when Wordsworth died in 1850. The richness of his imagery shows the influence of Keats, though his musical rhythms are very much his own. Tennyson wrote many famous poems, including 'The Lady of Shalott' and 'The Kraken'. He died in 1892 and is buried in Westminster Abbey.

Tennyson's poem, 'The Kraken', describes a beast that lives under the sea.

The Kraken

Below the thunders of the upper deep;
Far far beneath in the abysmal sea,
His ancient, dreamless, uninvaded sleep
The Kraken sleepeth: faintest sunlights flee
About his shadowy sides: above him swell
Huge sponges of millennial growth and height;
And far away into the sickly light,
From many a wondrous grot and secret cell
Unnumber'd and enormous polypi
Winnow with giant fins the slumbering green.
There hath he lain for ages and will lie
Battening upon huge seaworms in his sleep,
Until the latter fire shall heat the deep;
Then once by men and angels to be seen,
In roaring he shall rise and on the surface die.

Alfred, Lord Tennyson

Introduction

 Write a paragraph explaining the kind of creature you think Tennyson's Kraken is.

Make a drawing of what you imagine the Kraken looks like.

 Find three lines in the poem which best describe where the Kraken lives. What pictures are formed in your mind when you read the lines?

Can you think of a mythical beast that people believe in today that is similar to the Kraken? What does this say about people's imaginations?

Development

Read the following words and try to guess what they mean: 'abysmal', 'millennial', 'grot', 'polypi', 'winnow' and 'battening'.

Find the line where each word appears and try to make sense of it by reading the words that accompany it. Words that go before and after are called the **context**. Looking at a word in context like this means seeing how the words around it are able to add to its meaning. Check if your definitions were correct by looking in a dictionary.

 Tennyson wrote this poem over a hundred years ago. Read it again and think about the language he uses. Make a list of words which show that the poem was written long ago, then try to find a modern-day version.

FACT FILE

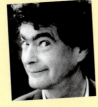

Brian Patten was born in 1946 in Liverpool where he was brought up. An award-winning poet, he has published many adult collections, and also writes poems for children. Patten is one of the Liverpool Poets, together with Roger McGough and Adrian Henri. Patten's work has been translated into many languages.

In 'A Small Dragon', the mythical beast is found in the speaker's woodshed. It is an astonishing find, and the poem, like 'The Kraken', is quite magical.

A Small Dragon

I've found a small dragon in the woodshed.
Think it must have come from deep inside a forest
because it's damp and green and leaves
are still reflecting in its eyes.

I fed it on many things, tried grass,
the roots of stars, hazel-nut and dandelion,
but it stared up at me as if to say, I need
foods you can't provide.

It made a nest among the coal,
not unlike a bird's but larger,
it is out of place here
and is quite silent.

If you believed in it I would come
hurrying to your house to let you share my wonder,
but I want instead to see
if you yourself will pass this way.

Brian Patten

1 Introduction

Brian Patten's dragon is a very different 'beast' from the one created by Tennyson. What are the thoughts that first spring into your mind about this creature?

Why does the speaker say he won't tell anybody about the dragon, but instead will wait to see if they pass his house?

How might Patten's dragon be compared to something else that is important and magical to us that we do not tell people about? Try to think of a time you kept a secret because you thought people might spoil it. Why would this have happened?

2 Development

Copy the following star diagrams into your book and find an appropriate line in the poems to complete them.

The Kraken lives...
'Far far beneath in the abysmal sea'

Kraken

- What does the creature spend its time doing?
- Which words suggest that the light might be bad for the Kraken?
- What will happen to the Kraken one day?

made a nest among the coal

A Small Dragon

- What had the dragon made for itself?
- Where does the speaker think the dragon has come from, and why?
- Does the dragon make any sound?
- What does the speaker try to feed his small dragon?
- Which line suggests that the speaker thinks people would never believe him?
- Which lines make you think the speaker's story is true?
- What do you think the poet's message is in the last four lines of the poem?

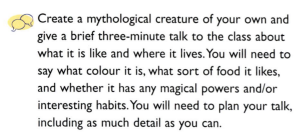 Create a mythological creature of your own and give a brief three-minute talk to the class about what it is like and where it lives. You will need to say what colour it is, what sort of food it likes, and whether it has any magical powers and/or interesting habits. You will need to plan your talk, including as much detail as you can.

 ## Plenary

Reread the aims at the start of the unit and think about how you have reached the targets while studying the poems. Answer the following questions:

- If a word seems obscure, how might reading it in context help?
- What do you notice about the language used in the poem by Tennyson compared to that of the poem by Patten?
- What are the main differences in the two mythical creatures? Look at lines from the poems for your answer.

 ## Homework

Using the library or the internet, research one of the mythical beasts that came up in the Starter exercise. Write a paragraph on the following:

- Where does the creature live and what special powers does it have?
- What is the story behind it? Where does the myth come from?
- Why have you chosen this particular beast? What do you find interesting about it?

Foxes

AIMS

- To understand rhythm and how it adds to the meaning of poetry;
- To explore how repetition can be useful for emphasis;
- To make meaningful comparisons between a pre- and post-1914 poem sharing a similar theme.

1 Starter

 Talk as a class about why a fox might be an interesting animal to write a story or poem about. Try to remember any stories or poems you know which contain foxes. What kind of 'personalities' are foxes normally given?

FACT FILE

John Clare was born in 1793 and was self-educated. He worked as a farm labourer, and loved the countryside and rural life. His poems are mainly about country life, and he has been described as a 'ploughman poet'. His work has been celebrated for capturing what rural life was really like in the nineteenth century.

This poem can be described as a **narrative** poem (narrative is another word for a story). In 'The Fox', John Clare is telling us a story.

The Fox

The shepherd on his journey heard when nigh
His dog among the bushes barking high;
The ploughman ran and gave a hearty shout,
He found a weary fox and beat him out.
The ploughman laughed and would have
  ploughed him in,
But the old shepherd took him for the skin.
He lay upon the furrow stretched for dead,
The old dog lay and licked the wounds that bled,
The ploughman beat him till his ribs would crack,
And then the shepherd slung him at his back;
And when he rested, to his dog's surprise,
The old fox started from his dead disguise
And while the dog lay panting on his sedge
He up and snapt and bolted through the hedge.

He scampered to the bushes far away;
The shepherd called the ploughman to the fray;
The ploughman wished he had a gun to shoot.
The old dog barked and followed the pursuit.
The shepherd threw his hook and tottered past;
The ploughman ran, but none could go so fast;
The woodman threw his faggot from the way
And ceased to chop and wondered at the fray.
But when he saw the dog and heard the cry
He threw his hatchet – but the fox was by.
The shepherd broke his hook and lost the skin;
He found a badger-hole and bolted in.
They tried to dig, but, safe from danger's way,
He lived to chase the hounds another day.

John Clare

Introduction

 With a partner, each read a stanza of the poem, then discuss the story.

- Why does the shepherd want the fox?
- What does the fox do?
- Who are the other characters in this poem?
- What do they do to try to catch the fox? Who wins?

Development

Notice how the lively pace and rhythm keeps the reader hooked into the tale. The fast pace also helps to build a sense of excitement, as we want to know what happens next. The rhythm helps the story to rattle towards its climax. See how the rhythm is created:

The / plough / man / ran / and / gave / a / heart / y / shout,

He / found / a / wear / y / fox / and / beat / him / out.

These lines from the poem have been broken up into single units of sound called **syllables**. The word 'mat' is a one-syllable word. 'Matter' (mat/ter) is a two-syllable word.

In the poem there are ten syllables in each line, which is the same length throughout the poem. The words are all either one or two syllables long. Using the same number of syllables in each line creates a regular, repetitive pattern in the poem. This makes the **rhythm** of the poem. The word 'rhythm' comes from the Greek word meaning 'flowing'. Here it is used to describe the sense of movement, or beat, in a poem. **Pace** describes how fast or slow that movement is.

 Read the poem again and, where appropriate, use the words 'syllable', 'rhythm' and 'pace' to answer the following questions.

- What is the rhythm in 'The Fox' like?
- What is the effect of using short words?
- The 'active' verbs chosen by the poet add to the poem's pace. Make a list of the verbs used to describe the movement of the fox.
- What kind of movement do they suggest? (Remember, a verb is a 'doing' word.)

FACT FILE

Ted Hughes was born in 1930 in Mytholroyd, Yorkshire, and died in 1998 in Devon. In 1948, he won a scholarship to study in Cambridge. Ted Hughes has published many collections of poetry and is mainly viewed as a Nature poet. He became Poet Laureate in 1984.

The Thought-Fox

I imagine this midnight moment's forest:
Something else is alive
Beside the clock's loneliness
And the blank page where my fingers move.

Through the window I see no star:
Something more near
Though deeper within darkness
Is entering the loneliness:

Cold, delicately as the dark snow
A fox's nose touches twig, leaf;
Two eyes serve a movement, that now
And again now, and now, and now

Sets neat prints into the snow
Between trees, and warily a lame
Shadow lags by stump and in hollow
Of a body that is bold to come

Across clearings, an eye,
A widening deepening greenness,
Brilliantly, concentratedly,
Coming about its own business

Till, with a sudden sharp hot stink of fox
It enters the dark hole of the head.
The window is starless still; the clock ticks,
The page is printed.

Ted Hughes

Introduction

In groups, talk about what you think is happening in this poem and make notes to answer the questions below. Rehearse your answers to feedback to the class.

■ What time of day is it?

■ What is the narrator doing?

■ Can he hear anything?

■ How would you describe the atmosphere in this poem?

■ What is the fox like? How does Hughes describes its appearance and movements?

■ Think carefully about the title of this poem. Why do you think this fox is a 'thought-fox'?

■ By the end of the poem, the 'blank page' has been printed. What does the page contain?

■ 'Two eyes serve a movement, that now
And again now, and now, and now'

Ted Hughes has purposefully repeated the word 'now'. Repetition like this can add emphasis, and Hughes is trying to draw our attention to something. What is it he is trying to emphasise?

Development

 Make notes about the foxes created by each of the poets. Which particular aspects of the animal does each of them cover best?

	The Fox	The Thought-Fox
The way the fox is described		
The way the fox moves/acts		
What the fox is doing		

What have you learned about how poets can use language to bring an animal to life?

How does the rhyme scheme of 'The Fox' add to the poem?

How has each poet created a sense of excitement and tension in his poem?

Try to explain the attitude of both poets to the fox about which they are writing.

Homework

Each poet gives his fox a different character. Write a couple of paragraphs explaining which you liked best and why.

or

Using an animal of your own choice, create a plan to help you write a poem of your own. Consider the following:

- What particular aspects of its character would you want to explore?
- Make a list of the verbs you would like to use to describe its movements.
- Think about how you could use rhyme or repetition in your poem for emphasis.

Using the plan you have put together, write a poem about the animal you have chosen.

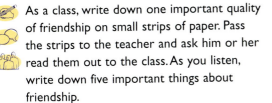

Friendship & Loyalty

AIMS

- To explore how form – rhyme scheme, free verse, etc. – is related to content;
- To understand symbols in poetry;
- To compare different kinds of friendships.

1 Starter

As a class, write down one important quality of friendship on small strips of paper. Pass the strips to the teacher and ask him or her read them out to the class. As you listen, write down five important things about friendship.

FACT FILE

Elizabeth Jennings was born in 1926 in Boston, Lincolnshire. Jennings likes regular verse forms and writes on themes of childhood, love and spiritual experience. She has written many adult collections and has also done translations and books of poems for children.

Elizabeth Jennings writes about the sort of friend someone might like to have, and creates her poem in steady rhymes which hold the reader's attention.

Friends

I fear it's very wrong of me,
And yet I must admit,
When someone offers friendship
I want the *whole* of it.
I don't want everybody else
To share my friends with me.
At least, I want *one* special one,
Who, indisputably

Likes me much more than all the rest,
Who's always on my side,
Who never cares what others say,
Who lets me come and hide
Within his shadow, in his house –
It doesn't matter where –
Who lets me simply be myself,
Who's always, *always* there.

Elizabeth Jennings

2 Introduction

With a partner, discuss the lines: 'When someone offers friendship/I want the *whole* of it' and 'Likes me much more than all the rest,/Who's always on my side'.

How important is it that a friend likes you best and is always on your side? This is the way we like to think of a friend, but is Elizabeth Jennings making us consider it more seriously?

Consider the following questions and be prepared to share your opinions with the class:

- What are the things that you expect from your friends?
- What does real friendship consist of?
- Should a real friend always be on your side, no matter what?
- Is it selfish or unreasonable to 'want the whole' of someone?

3 Development

The poem is in two stanzas of eight lines. Read the poem to each other in groups. Using clues from the poem, try to describe what you think the speaker is like. (Look, for example, at the number of times 'I', 'me' and 'myself' appear.) Is the age of the speaker suggested in the poem?

Now look at the poet's use of rhyme. Which of the lines rhyme? What sort of rhythm does it give the poem? Is it fast, slow, hesitant or demanding, strong or weak? How does the length of the lines add to this effect?

Does the use of rhyme help you to get a picture of the speaker in the poem? If so, why?

Scan the poem to find which word appears most in the first stanza and which in the second. How does this tell you the poem's **theme** is loyalty whilst its title is 'Friends'? Remember, the theme is what a poem is mainly about.

Love and Friendship

Love is like the wild rose briar,
Friendship, like the holly tree
The holly is dark when the rose briar blooms,
But which will bloom most constantly?

The wild rose briar is sweet in spring,
Its summer blossoms scent the air
Yet wait till winter comes again
And who will call the wild-briar fair?

Then scorn the silly rose-wreath now
And deck thee with the holly's sheen
That when December blights thy brow
He still may leave thy garland green-

Emily Jane Brontë

1 Introduction

 Discuss the following questions in groups and make notes on your conclusions.

 Using a thesaurus, look up the words 'constant' and 'fickle' and make a list of synonyms. What is Emily Brontë trying to say in her poem? Reread the poem and see if the words you have listed help you to understand it better.

With a partner, discuss how feelings can sometimes be compared with what you see in the natural world, i.e. what sort of feelings are associated with lightning or rain? See if you can link a piece of wood or a pebble from the beach with an emotion or feeling.

2 Development

 Thinking about the notes you have made, answer the following using full sentences.

- Give three ways in which 'love' might be seen as a 'wild rose briar'.

- Holly is an evergreen. Why could it be seen to be more lasting than the wild rose briar and, in Emily Brontë's eyes, more like friendship than love?

- Using a dictionary, look up the words 'fair', 'scorn', 'deck', 'blights', 'thy' and 'brow'. Write down what they mean. Are they still used today and, if so, how often? Has their meaning changed since the nineteenth century? Which words might be used today to mean the same thing?

The third poem, by John Burnside, is about 'possible' friendship. This time the friendship is with someone unknown who has never been seen.

FACT FILE

John Burnside has published three novels and seven books of poetry, of which the most recent, 'The Asylum Dance', won the Whitbread Poetry Prize.

A Pen Friend

A child's imagining,
that someone could be twinned
across those miles,
tuned to the same dark channel
of guesswork and song,

a real-time instance of myself
achieved elsewhere,
a boy in fishmonger's stripes
with milt on his fingers
or caked blood under his nails,

a mutuality
of love and fear,
similar patience, identical maps and toys,
the horse in each attic
awake in the motherless dark.

John Burnside

Burnside's poem is written in free verse in five-line stanzas. The poem does not rhyme but is, instead, carried along by its rhythms. Like many of his poems, although it is written in a simple, straightforward style, it is full of imagery and mysterious ideas.

1 Introduction

With a partner, discuss the hoped-for qualities of a pen friend and write a list of the five most important things. How do they compare with what the poet says? Be prepared to read your list to the class.

2 Development

With a partner, reread the poem and make notes on the following:

- What is meant by the phrases 'tuned to the same dark channel/of guesswork and song' and 'a real-time instance of myself'.
- Who is the boy in 'fishmonger's stripes'?
- What does it mean to have 'a mutuality/of love and fear' with another person? Find the word 'mutual' in a dictionary and see if it helps you to understand this question.
- What impression is given by the word 'dark' in the first and last stanzas?
- Would the effect be different if the horse in the attic was 'asleep' instead of 'awake'? Can you say how?
- Using the words 'guesswork and song' in a 'dark channel' make me think of life as…

The words used reveal much about the personality of the person who is speaking in the poem. Using the notes you have made, write as detailed a description of this person as you can. Think about the following questions to help you:

- Who and where are they?
- What has happened to them and are they happy or sad?

Use as much evidence from the text as you can to support your answer.

3 Plenary

In what ways is 'A Pen Friend' different from the other two poems in the unit?

Jennings talks of a 'shadow', whilst Brontë talks of the 'dark' holly, and Burnside has a 'dark channel' and 'the motherless dark' in his poem. Look for the words 'shadow', 'dark', 'channel' and 'motherless' in a thesaurus and make flow charts of similar words from what you find. Why might words like these be found in a poem about needing friends?

Do you agree with Emily Brontë that friendship can be trusted more than love?

How is the language used in the Brontë poem different from that of the others? Why you think this is?

4 Homework

Write a letter to an imaginary pen friend, telling them what you are like and how you like to spend your free time with your friends. Describe in detail the kind of hobbies that you and your friends enjoy, including a description of one or two or your friends to explain why you get on. What do you have in common?

Check your letter carefully. In case you need to redraft it, exchange it with a partner for discussion. This is part of the **process**. The process is what happens to your work along the way. The **product** is what you arrive at when you have made your best effort.

or

Go back to the five most important qualities in friendship that you listed at the beginning of the unit and explain why each of these is important.

Space

AIMS

- To reinforce knowledge of free verse, rhyming couplets, imagery and theme as applied to poetry;

- To compare how three poets have looked at the idea of space;

- To compare poetic forms and look at their suitability for the content of a given poem;

- To find words used in poetry from pre-1914 and attempt to find their equivalent in today's language;

- To think about how the way we express ourselves changes over time.

1 Starter

Imagine that you had the opportunity to go into space for a year, leaving your friends behind. Would you want to go? In groups, list five things that you would like to do if you could travel in space, five things you would miss about Earth while you were away, and five luxury items you would take with you.

FACT FILE

Patrick Brontë was born in Ireland in 1777 and was father to the famous Brontë children: Charlotte, Emily, Anne and Patrick. Patrick Brontë died in 1861 aged 85, outliving all his family.

From: On Halley's Comet

Our blazing guest, long have you been,
To us, and many more, unseen;
Full seventy years have pass'd away
Since last we saw you, fresh and gay –
Time seems to do you little wrong –
As yet, you sweep the sky along,
A thousand times more glib and fast,
Than railroad speed or sweeping blast –
Not so – the things you left behind –
Not so – the race of human kind,
Vast changes in this world have been,
Since by this world you last were seen:
The child who clapped his hands with joy,
And hailed thee as a shining toy,
Has pass'd long since, that dusky bourn,
From whence no travellers return;
Or sinking now in feeble age,
Surveys thee, as a hoary sage;
Sees thee, a mighty globe serene,
Wide hurried o'er the welkin sheen…

Patrick Brontë

Patrick Brontë's poem is written about a real event in the late nineteenth century. Brontë has used the arrival of the comet to look at changes in the passage of time.

Introduction

 In your groups, discuss the following questions and make notes on your ideas. Be prepared to feed them back to the class.

- How long is it since the comet was last seen?
- What does Brontë mean when he says time does the comet 'little wrong'?
- What does he compare it with that might be more harmful?
- Why do you think the poet refers to the comet as a 'shining toy' at one point in the poem?
- What might the child referred to see the comet as now?
- The comet is called a 'guest'. What is Brontë trying to get across?

Make a list of all the changes Brontë says have occurred since the comet last appeared.

Development

 Write down what you think is meant by the words: 'dusky bourn', 'whence', 'hoary sage', 'serene' and 'welkin sheen'. Some of the words can still be found in a dictionary. Look them up and see how close you were.

 Using the notes you have made, write a paragraph on:

- what Patrick Brontë thinks about the comet;
- what he thinks about the passing of time.

In the second poem, Tim Kendall writes about astronauts and space travel; a subject most of us have daydreamed about.

FACT FILE

Tim Kendall was born in Plymouth in 1970. He now lives in Wiltshire and teaches at the university of Bristol. As well as writing his own poetry, Tim Kendall is also editor of the magazine, 'Thumbscrew'.

Astronauts

The earliest astronauts
understood the risks:
they'd always half expected

God to swat
their overreaching craft.
When nothing of note occurred,

they carried back
for analysis
a punnet of blackest space,

which the scientists
laser-blasted to conclude
that God did not exist.

The astronauts' confidence grew.
Soon they were
tailgating comets,

marvelling
that man should be
so impudent, so great.

Amidst the worldwide
carnival, a veteran
began to recall

how he'd felt homesick
not for his little town
nor for his state or nation,

but for a planet
he could blot out
with his thumb.

Tim Kendall

1 Introduction

 Read the poem to yourself, then, with a partner, discuss the following lines:

 'they'd always half expected
 God to swat
their overreaching craft.'

and

'a punnet of blackest space,'

Why is the craft referred to as 'overreaching'?

What sort of image does the poet create of God and man?

Were the astronauts afraid of some sort of supernatural intervention?

 Make notes of other worries the astronauts might have had when entering space in early times.

2 Development

 In groups, discuss the following questions and make notes. Be prepared to feedback your answers to the class.

Why do you think that the astronauts' confidence grew when they thought they'd discovered that God did not exist? How did it affect their attitude to space travel?

The verses have been arranged into short three-line stanzas. Why do you think this has been done and what effect does it have? Does the shape of the poem suggest anything to you?

What do you understand by the word 'veteran'? Why might the carnival or circus atmosphere be less important than something else mentioned at the end of the poem? What do you think that was?

 An increase in scientific knowledge has meant that life has changed considerably. Make a list of as many recent inventions as you can think of that have become a common sight in today's world.

Choose one item from your list and write a paragraph about all the advantages this invention has brought, explaining why the world would be a poorer place without it.

Now choose another item and write a paragraph explaining why this invention has had a negative effect on the world (perhaps by causing pollution or disease, etc.).

The final poem, " 'Do You Think We'll Ever Get to See Earth, Sir?' " by Sheenagh Pugh, explores the possibility of having to leave our planet because it has become uninhabitable.

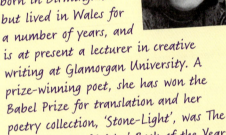

FACT FILE

Sheenagh Pugh was born in Birmingham but lived in Wales for a number of years, and is at present a lecturer in creative writing at Glamorgan University. A prize-winning poet, she has won the Babel Prize for translation and her poetry collection, 'Stone-Light', was The Arts Council of Wales' Book of the Year.

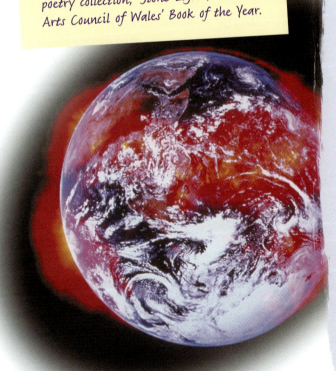

'Do You Think We'll Ever Get to See Earth, Sir?'

I hear they're hoping to run trips
one day, for the young and fit, of course.
I don't see much use in it myself;
there'll be any number of places
you can't land, because they're still toxic,
and even in the relatively safe bits
you won't see what it was, what it could be.
I can't fancy a tour through the ruins
of my home with a party of twenty-five
and a guide to tell me what to see.
But if you should see some beautiful thing,
some leaf, say, damascened with frost,
some iridescence on a pigeon's neck,
some stone, some curve, some clear water,
look at it as if you were made of eyes,
as if you were nothing but an eye, lidless
and tender, to be probed and scorched
by extreme light. Look at it with your skin,
with the small hairs on the back of your neck.
If it is well-shaped, look at it with your hands;
if it has fragrance, breathe it into yourself;
if it tastes sweet, put your tongue to it.
Look at it as a happening, a moment;
let nothing of it go unrecorded,
map it as if it were already passing.
Look at it with the inside of your head,
look at it for later, look at it for ever,
and look at it once for me.

Sheenagh Pugh

1 Introduction

Work with a partner to make notes on the following:

- List the images in the poem and divide them into two columns: the Earth as the teacher remembers it, and as it is after it had to be abandoned.

- Scan the poem, making a note of the number of times that the teacher tells his or her students to 'look at it' and memorise what they see. What is the effect of this? What does it suggest about the environment inhabited by humans after the Earth has been abandoned?

- " 'Do You Think We'll Ever Get to See Earth, Sir?' " is written in free verse. Write down whether or not you think this is a suitable form for the content of the poem.

- Copy out the lines that best describe the importance of time, and how vital it is to appreciate its beauty there and then.

- Why does the speaker end with the words, 'and look at it once for me'? What does he or she expect from such a statement?

2 Development

Make a list of what is most important to you on Earth that you would miss if you were forced to live in space. Then list the things you'd be glad to leave behind.

Now write a letter as if you had just arrived from another planet and must tell the folks back home what you have seen and experienced on Earth.

3 Plenary

Using the following paragraph openers, see what you have learned from the poems, and find out if you have hit your initial targets:

- Modern words I would use to say 'the welkin sheen' are…

- The stanzas in 'Astronauts' that suggest similar ideas to 'or sinking now in feeble age,/Surveys thee, as a hoary sage;/Sees thee, a mighty globe serene,' are…

- In his poem, Patrick Brontë talks of changes having occurred since the comet was last seen. Some of the changes I have seen in my own lifetime are…

- The line in 'Astronauts' that suggests humans are not as innocent as the comet, when blasting through space, is…

- The solid free verse block of writing for " 'Do You Think We'll Ever Get to See Earth, Sir?' " reminds us of…

4 Homework

Each of the three poems looks at time, progress, and space in a different way. Choose two of the three poems and compare and contrast what the poets have to say about these issues. Do they hold the same views? Make sure you use the notes you made earlier before answering.

or

Choose one of the technological changes you have seen in your lifetime and write about how it has affected you personally.

The Moon

- To consider how poets use words to create links to other ideas in our minds;
- To explore how language can be used to create vivid pictures and to reinforce knowledge of metaphor;
- To develop confidence and ability to search for layers of meaning in poems;
- To use talk as a way of sharing views and expanding your own ideas;
- To use a thesaurus to expand vocabulary;
- To give a three-minute talk to the class.

In this unit you will work through 'The Morning Moon' by Derek Walcott, and 'Wolf Man' by Wendy Bardsley. Although both poems are about the moon, they are approached from different perspectives.

1 Starter

 As a class, brainstorm the subjects that might be covered in poems about the moon. Talk about the titles of the two poems in this unit. What do they tell you about the poems?

FACT FILE

Derek Walcott was born in St Lucia, and educated at St Mary's College and the University of the West Indies. He has taught at the universities of Columbia, Yale and Harvard, and is currently Professor of English at Boston University. He has published many poetry collections and plays and was awarded The Nobel Prize for Literature in 1992.

The Morning Moon

Still haunted by the cycle of the moon
racing full sail
past the crouched whale's back of Morne Coco Mountain,

I gasp at her sane brightness.

It's early December,
the breeze freshens the skin of this earth,
the goose-skin of water,

and I notice the blue plunge
of shadows down Morne Coco Mountain,
December's sundial,

happy that the earth is still changing,
that the full moon can blind me with her forehead
this bright foreday morning,

and that fine sprigs of white are springing from my beard.

Derek Walcott

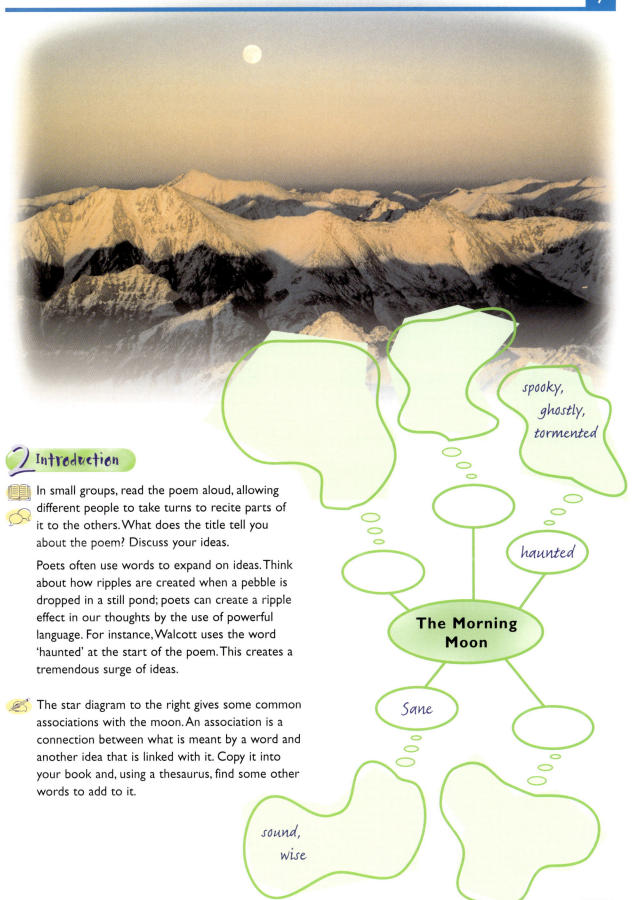

Introduction

In small groups, read the poem aloud, allowing different people to take turns to recite parts of it to the others. What does the title tell you about the poem? Discuss your ideas.

Poets often use words to expand on ideas. Think about how ripples are created when a pebble is dropped in a still pond; poets can create a ripple effect in our thoughts by the use of powerful language. For instance, Walcott uses the word 'haunted' at the start of the poem. This creates a tremendous surge of ideas.

The star diagram to the right gives some common associations with the moon. An association is a connection between what is meant by a word and another idea that is linked with it. Copy it into your book and, using a thesaurus, find some other words to add to it.

spooky, ghostly, tormented

haunted

The Morning Moon

Sane

sound, wise

3 Development

Find the verbs in Walcott's poem that give it movement and life. One of them is 'racing' in the first stanza. Can you find some others?

What is the image Walcott gives us of the Morne Coco Mountain in the first stanza? Why is this a metaphor and not a simile? Why should he use this particular image? Look at the lines that come before it.

To see how similes and metaphors can be used to describe special qualities, copy the diagram below into your book and complete it. An example of a metaphor has been done for you.

> Using what is called a **simile** to make a comparison can be very effective. A simile is different from a **metaphor** in that the word 'as' or 'like' is used to compare things. A metaphor does not do this, but just says something is something else (even though this is not literally true).
>
> Simile: The swan passed like a white cloud on the water.
>
> Metaphor: The white cloud of a swan paused in the water.

Scenery/landscape	The special qualities I am trying to capture are...	Comparison
The night sky	The dazzling stars	The black jewelled gown of the night sky
A mountain		
An iceberg		
A desert		

FACT FILE

Wendy Bardsley has worked widely as a teacher and has also been a university lecturer. She writes for adults, young people and children, and has published four poetry collections, two anthologies and several works of non-fiction for use in education.

Wolfman

I heard your warped cry in the night,
Stopping my ears;
A screech of beast,
That twist of passion missed by man,
That fierce taboo you knew you must have.

You hid your curved fingernails,
Your lengthening teeth, the fur,
Growing indiscreetly
On the back of your hands.

And for a time you tried to fool your senses,
Soft skies, gentle pastoral scenes, your game,
Avoiding the glare of the seething moon.
I knew you first a legend,
Cruel with beauty. Such was your appeal.

I pace your grave-yard horror now,
Feel your fervour in the darkening air,
Stare, and wonder where you are,
On the other side of sunlight.

Wendy Bardsley

Introduction

 Below are some words from 'Wolfman'. Copy the chart into your book and find the words in a thesaurus. Complete the lists of synonyms. The first has been done for you.

warped	*twisted, crooked, wrenched, corrupted, tortured, monstrous...*
screech	_____
taboo	_____
seething	_____
cruel	_____
fervour	

 Having completed your chart, reread the poem.
 How would you describe the atmosphere?
Discuss your ideas with your group.

 **Development**

 How does the moon in 'Wolfman' contrast with that in 'The Morning Moon'? Discuss the following questions in your groups and make notes of your answers. Be prepared to discuss your answers as a class.

- How is the moon described in 'The Morning Moon'?
- What does the moon mean to the 'Wolfman'?
- Who is the narrator (the person who is speaking) in each poem? In 'Wolfman' what is the narrator's relationship with the Wolfman?
- What exactly is the narrator in 'The Morning Moon' admiring about the moon?

Discuss how the poet might be feeling in 'The Morning Moon' when 'fine sprigs of white are springing' from his beard. How effective is the word 'springing' here at the end of the poem?

 **Plenary**

In what way does using a powerful word to trigger associations make poetry more effective?

Explain the difference between a simile and a metaphor. How does using an image to compare and expand ideas help create a more vivid poem?

As well as just describing the moon, these poems contain other thoughts and messages. Can you find any of them?

 **Homework**

Using the library or the internet, research any myths or legends you know of that are associated with the moon. Make notes on what you find and prepare a three-minute talk to tell the class about your research.

Earth

AIMS

- To work through three poems about the Earth by poets from different cultures;

- To make good use of a dictionary and a thesaurus;

- To learn about the individual power of words and how they can appeal to the senses;

- To see how repetition and patterns of sound add strength to lines in a poem;

- To reinforce knowledge of imagery and empathy;

- To understand synonyms and antonyms.

1 Starter

In the following poems, Earth is explored in three very different ways. The first poem is about the life of a worm, deep down in the soil. In the second poem, the ground suddenly starts to break up in an earthquake; while the third describes Earth's beauty, and the sights and sounds of dawn.

As a class, talk about the living things you might find in the earth. Discuss the power of the Earth and how you feel when you hear about earthquakes and volcanoes. Write down four things about the Earth that you think are beautiful. Feedback your ideas to the class. Are any of them surprising?

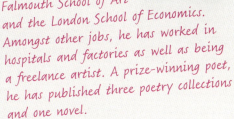

FACT FILE

Gerard Woodward was born in north London in 1961. He studied at Falmouth School of Art and the London School of Economics. Amongst other jobs, he has worked in hospitals and factories as well as being a freelance artist. A prize-winning poet, he has published three poetry collections and one novel.

In this poem, a worm is acting as narrator and telling us what he thinks about 'dirt' – that is, his own habitat.

Worm

Dirt is myth.
This we learn
In our brown studies.

Dirt is house
Hearth and latch-key,
Mouth-shaped. Spat out.

Dirt is nakedness.
Where sunlight is vague.
Where rain is slow.

Dirt is roots.
Vegetation's beginnings,
Buildings' unpalatable foundations.

Dirt is history.
We hear all
Its footfalls.

Gerard Woodward

Introduction

 Dirt is often thought of in a negative way. Look up the word in a dictionary and thesaurus and create a list of **synonyms**. Then, when you have done this, do the same thing for these words from the poem:

- myth
- hearth
- roots
- history

 Looking at the word lists you have created, compare the list of synonyms you have made for 'dirt' with the others. Can you draw any conclusions? Reread the poem. What is the worm saying?

Development

In this poem, Gerard Woodward has the worm talking directly to us. When creatures and things are made to speak, move or act like humans, it is known as **personification**. Working with a partner, copy out the two lines that tell us the worm is speaking.

 Now answer the following questions on the poem. Make notes and be prepared to discuss your answers.

Look at the pattern of sounds. Note how each stanza begins 'Dirt is'. What is the effect of this repetition?

What is meant by the lines:
'Dirt is myth.'
'Dirt is house/Hearth and latch-key,/Mouth-shaped. Spat out.'
'Dirt is nakedness./Where sunlight is vague.'
'Dirt is history.'

Discuss your responses with a partner. Make notes on your conclusions.

> When we identify with the life of another creature or person, we **empathise** with them. Empathy is when we try to imagine what it is like to be someone or something else.

 Using the notes you have made, write a paragraph each on how people might usually think about dirt and how the earthworm in the poem challenges these ideas.

Then, using one of the following words, create a short poem of your own:

- rose
- fire
- stone
- tree

Write it in three stanzas, applying the repetition you have seen in 'Worm'. Try to think of something different and surprising to say for each stanza.

Here is an example:

Rose is red.
This is not shown
in its seed.

Rose is fragrant.
Bouquets are made from the imagination of people.

Roses do not know of beauty.
They are sometimes eaten by insects.

FACT FILE

Bibhu Padhi was born in 1951. He has published several books of poetry and is also a translator and a writer of non-fiction. He teaches English at SCS College, in Puri, India, where he lives with his wife and two sons.

Bibhu Padhi's poem, 'The Earthquake', shows how the earth is its own master and can sometimes function in ways that frighten us. Padhi wrote this poem almost immediately after an earthquake had struck Cuttack.

The Earthquake

The morning it arrived

we looked at our costly watches,
wondered at the rare miscalculation of
the town's usually efficient astrologer.

We traced its humble origin
to acts of pride and violence
committed a long time ago.

We told ourselves: 'There are
other worlds yet, other space,
where human beings can find

sufficient room
for all the many sins
of the body and the soul.'

We felt the insidious
vibration of God's anger
at our poor little doorsteps.

In a fit of human rage, we promised
to build houses that'll keep their cool
during sly unsympathetic weather.

We came out of our homes and saw
the planets giving birth
to other, larger planets.

We said: 'After this invasion of faith,
mankind shall learn to stand
erect and upright again;

once again God shall ascend
our ill-lit altars
and allow us to pray.'

That evening, while we were trying
to gather up our exploded faith,
we saw the stars and the moon in tears.

We sat down and prayed.

Bibhu Padhi

Introduction

 This poem concerns a community's reaction to an earthquake and the ways in which society struggles to make sense of the natural disaster.

Words can reinforce each other, both when they have the same or similar meaning, and when they are opposites. Remember, similar words are called **synonyms** and their opposites are called **antonyms**. Use a dictionary and a thesaurus to list antonyms for the following words from the poem. The first has been done for you.

- costly – *inexpensive, cheap, marked-down, half-price*
- humble
- rage
- ascend
- insidious

 One word to add to the bank of 'cheap' is 'worthless'. Notice how strong this opposite word is when you see how the poet has called the watches 'costly'. The word here is a kind of joke. Why do you think this is?

 Read the poem again and compare your lists of antonyms with the words the poet has used. What do they tell you about the people's reaction to the earthquake? What do they tell you about the people themselves?

Development

Now you have examined the words chosen by the poet, and the wider implications of these words, pick out the lines that suggest:

- the people's surprise at the power of the earthquake to destroy;
- the way the people excuse themselves from blame. Whose fault do they say it is?
- the lines that suggest that guilt is an important theme in the poem;
- the ways in which the people try to make sense of the destruction – why do they think it has happened?
- the lines which refer to the people's faith. What has happened to it?
- the way the poet conveys the rising sense of panic as the poem progresses.

 Write a paragraph on what you think each poet is saying about the power of the Earth and what he is saying about the power of humankind's scientific calculations. Use quotations from the poem wherever possible to support your ideas.

FACT FILE

Sun Yün-feng was born in Chekiang, China, in 1764, the daughter of an official. She later married a scholar called Ch'en and was one of the favourites of 13 women students of the Ch'ing Dynasty poet, Yüan Mei.

The third poem in this unit is by the Chinese poet, Sun Yün-feng, and it explores the Earth's natural beauty. The poem is rich in imagery and sensory detail.

Starting at Dawn

Under the waning moon
In the dawn –
A frosty bell.
My horse's hooves
Tramp through the yellow leaves.
As the sun rises
Not a human being is visible,
Only the sound of a stream
Through the misty trees.

Sun Yün-feng

(translated from Chinese by Kenneth Rexroth and Ling Chung)

1 Introduction

'Starting at Dawn' looks at the Earth in a very different way from the previous two poems. The poet is describing its beauty as she prepares for a journey at dawn, creating in words the sounds and sights she experiences.

Work with a partner to make a list of the sights and sounds listed in the poem.

Think about the images that come into your mind when you read the poem. Write a sentence to try to describe these three phrases:

'waning moon'

'frosty bell'

'misty trees'

2 Development

Sun Yün-feng creates a scene of beauty by thinking, looking and listening. Write five lines of your own, describing a beautiful scene from your memory. Perhaps it is something from a holiday, or the early morning or evening. Remember to include sights and sounds, and also scents if you can, to show how the dawn can affect the senses.

3 Plenary

Answer the following questions to see how many aims you have managed to target.

- Why might an earthquake seem like a punishment from God to people in certain parts of the world?
- What is it called when you have a worm (or any animal or thing) as the narrator in a piece of writing?
- What is the effect of the repetition in 'Worm' and 'The Earthquake'?
- What does 'synonym' mean?
- What does 'antonym' mean?

4 Homework

The three poems look at the idea of 'Earth' in different ways. Compare the ways in which all three are different, making sure that you consider:

- what each poem is about;
- how the ideas in the poem contrast (use quotations where you can to support what you say);
- which of the poems you like best and why.

Autumn

■ To see how poets use imagery to create powerful pictures in the minds of their readers;

■ To explore a pre-1914 ode and two contemporary poems to see how styles of writing have changed;

■ To understand atmosphere and mood;

■ To find out how poems, whilst sharing the same theme, can have different atmospheres;

■ To look at the way poets express their personal views and feelings, allowing their personalities to shape their work;

■ To learn about tone in poetry;

■ To compare and contrast three poems.

1 Starter

On strips of paper, write down four features of autumn that you find most striking and/or memorable. Use these to create a bank of words and ideas that the class can use to describe that season.

The following stanza is an extract from the famous ode 'To Autumn', written by Keats in September 1819. Note the formal style of the writing – this was the usual style of his day.

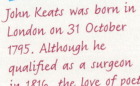

FACT FILE

John Keats was born in London on 31 October 1795. Although he qualified as a surgeon in 1816, the love of poetry was always with him and he became a professional writer – often very short of money but doing what he loved best for the rest of his short life. Keats died from consumption in 1821 when he was just 26 years old.

Keats is, perhaps, most famous for his **odes**. An ode is a way of praising a person or thing in written form, and in Unit 1, 'What is a Poem?', you saw a draft of his 'Ode to a Nightingale'.

From: To Autumn

Season of mists and mellow fruitfulness!
Close bosom-friend of the maturing sun;
Conspiring with him how to load and bless
With fruit the vines that round the thatch-eves run;
To bend with apples the moss'd cottage-trees,
And fill all fruit with ripeness to the core;
To swell the gourd, and plump the hazel shells
With a sweet kernel; to set budding more,
And still more, later flowers for the bees,
Until they think warm days will never cease,
For Summer has o'er-brimm'd their clammy cells.

John Keats

Introduction

 Make notes on the following and be prepared to discuss your answers. Poets often use 'word pictures' to stimulate our senses of sight, sound, smell, taste and touch. The sense experiences created this way are called **images**. Keats's ode 'To Autumn' can be described as being rich in imagery.

Reread the poem carefully. Pick out three examples of imagery that suggest that autumn is a season of calm and contentment.

Then look at the line that describes autumn as 'Close bosom-friend of the maturing sun'. What do these 'friends' plan to do?

Some people might feel that autumn is the end of summer and the beginning of winter. Why do you think that Keats might have written an ode to autumn rather than summer? Read the poem again before you note down your ideas.

Some of the words in Keats's poem belong to a bygone age. Working on your own, scan the lines and see if you can pick them out. Then find two more examples.

Pre-1914 word/s	Meaning	Modern-day version
bosom-friend	close friend	best friend/mate

 Development

 Keats adds movement to his poem by choosing active verbs that bring energy into the lines. With a partner, find the verbs 'run', 'bend' and 'swell', before picking out four more to add to the list.

The sound of words can play an important part in creating the tone of the poem. The tone might be called the **attitude** of the poem – that is, whether it is serious, playful, sombre, etc.

Read the first few lines carefully. (It will probably help to read them aloud.) Keats has repeatedly used certain sounds. How would you describe them? (Long, short, soft, harsh, slow, quick…) How do these words bring to mind the ripeness of autumn?

Now use your notes to write two paragraphs on how Keats has achieved a sense of contentment in the poem. Explain how certain words have been used to create rich imagery. Describe the atmosphere of the poem and the way it makes you feel.

In this second poem, Douglas Dunn uses imagery to create a very different view of autumn from that of Keats. Dunn is a contemporary poet and writes in a much less formal style than Keats, who wrote his poem over a hundred years earlier.

FACT FILE

Douglas Dunn was born and grew up in Renfrewshire. He was educated at The Scottish School of Librarianship and the University of Hull where he worked as a librarian. Dunn writes on themes of domesticity, class, nature and love with deep-felt honesty. He has published a wide range of work and is also a professor at the University of St Andrews.

Early Autumn

Last month, by this same window, moist dusks
Closed the light slowly by summer curtains
And the eye had its space to go flying
Through glassy corners of sky, land and water.

Now it is dark and mid-September breathes
Numberless whispers. After blue sky,
Still Firth and summer's dry appearances,
Night is quick, with shivers at its edges.

Moths in the lampshades set to their *maudit*
Radiant, nocturnal manias, last gasps,
Powdery suicides on whirring wings.
They drop dead from electric interrogations.

My fingers smell of a soap that is new to me.
I should close windows, but aromatic fires
Linger from stubble burning all over Fife
And nothing's left of black daylight smoke.

An insect scribbles its white signature.
The letter 'a' can be seen through a veined wing.
Through 'a' the beginning of time can be seen,
A serpent's tongue licking around an apple.

Something begins in me; but I don't know
What it is yet. I shall try to find out.
It could be some sort of inhuman benevolence
Made of moth-powder, wings, smoke and soap.

Douglas Dunn

Introduction

Discuss the following questions in pairs and make notes. Be prepared to discuss your answers with the class.

■ Notice the descriptions of movement the poet creates as autumn replaces summer. Make a list of all the changes Dunn is saying that autumn brings with it. How many can you find?

■ The poem is mainly about the passing of time, and the way one season turns into another. Look carefully at the fifth stanza. What is meant by these lines? 'Through 'a' the beginning of time can be seen, A serpent's tongue licking around an apple.'

■ Dunn is unsure what is happening to him in the last stanza. What do you think the last two lines mean?

■ Both Dunn and Keats have chosen words that appeal to our five senses (sight, sound, smell, taste and touch). Read the poems again and jot down any words that involve these senses. Copy and complete the chart below:

'To Autumn' by John Keats		'Early Autumn' by Douglas Dunn	
Word	Sense	Word	Sense
fruitfulness	taste	shivers	touch

Development

Read your notes, then compare the two poems. Try to include the following points in your writing:

■ The way the poems describe autumn;

■ The language used in the poems;

■ Which of the poems matches most with your own feelings about autumn;

■ Which you like best and why.

FACT FILE

John Hegley is a performance poet who studied at Bradford University then returned to London to work in children's theatre. He has performed at many venues around the country, including the Hackney Empire and the Bloomsbury Theatre, London.

His poem, 'Autumn Verses', uses **wordplay**. Wordplay is when poets use words in an unexpected way to create surprising, unusual or comical effects.

Autumn Verses

Autumn is strange stuff
anagram of Aunt mu
but not of nostalgia.

Scarves come out, clocks go back
faulty or otherwise,
pumpkins enjoy brief popularity.

Kids collecting cash
for slouched-on-the-ground
ash-bound bad dressers.

Ore tummy, heart of mould
old leaves leaving
enter the cold.

Last October
I got very depressed
when our dog got knoctober.

John Hegley

1 Introduction

  With a partner, discuss the following questions and make notes on your answers.

■ 'Autumn is strange stuff', says the poet. Why might Hegley find it 'strange'?

> Hegley uses the word 'stuff' at the start of his poem. This is a widely-used **colloquial** word, popular because it can be given whatever interpretation you like according to your own thoughts. A colloquial word is usually the kind of word you would use in conversation rather than prose.

■ 'Autumn' is not an anagram of 'nostalgia'. Why might Hegley point this out? What might he be nostalgic for?

■ The poet refers to specific dates in the year in the poem. What are they and how does Hegley refer to them?

Development

Hegley's poem is humorous. Read the other two poems again and try to find lines that show how the other poets feel about autumn. Judging from the poems, write a paragraph on how you think each poet feels about the season. Then, when you have done this, add a final paragraph on how *you* feel about the season. (You might like to use the bank of words that you compiled during the Starter exercise to help you.) Support your writing by using words from the poems. For example, you might begin:

I think Douglas Dunn likes/dislikes autumn because he says…

Plenary

- Keats's poem was written over a hundred years before the others. How can you tell this from the language?
- What do you understand by the terms 'tone', 'atmosphere' and 'mood' in poetry?
- How might a poet's personality be seen in their work?
- What do you look for when comparing and contrasting poems? (For example, language, grammar, humour, etc.)
- Can you find an example of wordplay in Hegley's poem? Write it down and note why it is funny.

Homework

The poems in this unit are all about the changes that happen in autumn. Choose another season and try to write about it in prose. Remember to paragraph your writing and to use complete sentences. (Prose is spoken or written language that is not condensed or formed into verse.) Try to explain how senses – sight, sounds, touch, smell and taste – have all enriched the poems.

or

Contrast the three poems by showing how they are different in tone and atmosphere. Remember that the tone is whether the poem is serious, playful, etc., whilst the atmosphere is more of an overall mood. For example, Hegley's tone is playful whilst the mood is nostalgic; Dunn's tone is serious and thoughtful; and Keats's tone is dignified though the mood is one of admiration and praise. Try to use the following words in your writing:

formal, informal, colloquial, serious, funny, complex, slang, pun, simple, clear, nostalgic.

Use a thesaurus and a dictionary to help you form your answers.

Birdsong

■ To contrast Romantic and contemporary poetry;

■ To focus on pre-1914 language;

■ To form judgements about style and content;

■ To compare poems.

Percy Bysshe Shelley was what is called a Romantic poet. The Romantic era refers to a time in the late eighteenth and early nineteenth centuries when there was an attempt by many writers, artists and musicians to break away from the old, formal rules and ways of thinking, and to develop modern, new ideas. Romantic poetry is associated with intense and imaginative feelings, trying to highlight the beauty of life and rebelling against cold scientific ideas.

1 Starter

The two poems in this unit have been inspired by sound. In the first, Shelley has captured the beauty of a skylark's song; while in the second, Seamus Heaney focuses on the harshness of bird songs – a very different response from that of Shelley. In small groups, talk about sounds you enjoy listening to and sounds you do not like. For instance, how might sound be considered 'pollution' or, in some cases, 'therapy'? Listen to and consider the opinions of others. Do you all agree? Make notes of your findings.

List five sounds that you like and five you hate. Be prepared to feed back your ideas to the class and to explain why you like/dislike the sounds. What do they mean to you?

FACT FILE

Percy Bysshe Shelley was educated at Eton and Oxford. A Romantic poet, Shelley wrote many poems that have become an important part of our literary heritage, as well as prose and plays. Sadly, he drowned when he was only 30 years old.

From: To a Skylark

Hail to thee, blithe Spirit!
Bird thou never wert,
That from heaven, or near it,
Pourest thy full heart
In profuse strains of unpremeditated art.

Higher still and higher
From the earth thou springest,
Like a cloud of fire,
The blue deep thou wingest,
And singing still dost soar, and soaring ever singest.

In the golden lightning
Of the sunken sun
O'er which clouds are bright'ning,
Thou dost float and run,
Like an unbodied joy whose race is just begun.

Percy Bysshe Shelley

Introduction

This poem was written in 1820. Reread the extract carefully and try to work out what the poet is saying in each line.

Then copy and complete the table below, noting those words and phrases that tell us that the poem was written in another century and 'translating' them into contemporary language.

How many words have you found that are no longer in use? What does this tell us about the way language changes over time? Compile your ideas as a group and be prepared to feed them back to class.

Words/phrases that tell us the poem was written in another century	Modern-day equivalent

Development

Shelley has tried to bring the image of the skylark to life by creating pictures of both sound and vision. Fill in a table of phrases that appeal to our sense of hearing and those that appeal to our sense of sight. For example:

Words which appeal to our sense of hearing	Words which appeal to our sense of vision
profuse strains	a cloud of fire

In 'Serenades', Seamus Heaney has something very different from Shelley to say about birds.

FACT FILE

Seamus Heaney's poetry often concerns rural life, how people change as they mature, and death. He searched for a way to relate thoughts and feelings about political events in Northern Ireland without becoming propagandist. He has published many poetry collections and, in 1995, was awarded the Nobel Prize for Poetry.

Serenades

The Irish nightingale
Is a sedge-warbler,
A little bird with a big voice
Kicking up a racket all night.

Not what you'd expect
From the musical nation.
I haven't even heard one –
Nor an owl, for that matter.

My serenades have been
The broken voice of a crow
In a draught or a dream,
The wheeze of bats

Or the ack-ack
Of the tramp corncrake
Lost in a no-man's-land
Between combines and chemicals.

So fill the bottles, love,
Leave them inside their cots,
And if they do wake us, well,
So would the sedge-warbler.

Seamus Heaney

1 Introduction

Discuss the questions below, making notes on your answers. Be prepared to present your ideas to the class.

- What is meant by the word 'serenade'? (You may need to look the word up in a dictionary.) What kinds of sounds could be thought of as serenades? Try to give three examples.

- What is Heaney saying about serenades? What sounds have been his own serenades? Find phrases used to describe the sounds he has heard.

- In his poem, Heaney is making a joke about sounds and serenades. He is 'sending up' the idea of the beauty of birdsong. This kind of humour in writing is called **irony**. Heaney is also using irony by calling his poem 'Serenades', as the sounds he goes on to describe are not serenades at all. For example:
  'So fill the bottles, love,
  Leave them inside their cots,'
  Who do you think Heaney talking to here? What is his message?

- In this poem, Heaney writes, at times, in an almost conversational style using words and phrases you might expect to hear in speech. Why might he have chosen to write this poem in an informal and 'chatty' style? How does it fit with what he is saying?

2 Development

Shelley and Heaney have very different views of the birds they are writing about. Shelley 'sings the praises' of the skylark, whilst Heaney describes the birdsong in his poem in a much more down-to-earth way.

In writing, first compare the language used by each of the poets when they describe the birds in their poems and then say what is different about it. Where possible, use quotations from the poems to support your ideas. Use the following paragraph openers to help you.

- Both Shelley and Heaney have used words that help their reader imagine the sounds that each bird makes. For example…

- However, the words Shelley uses tell us that…
- The tone of Shelley's poem is…
- This contrasts with the tone of Heaney's poem because…
- I prefer the poem… because…

3 Plenary

Explain how Shelley's style of writing is very different from that of Heaney's. What phrases does Shelley use to describe the song of the skylark? How many times does Shelley refer to 'heaven' in his poem? Why do you think he has made this link between the skylark and heaven?

4 Homework

Shelley's poem is a good example of a Romantic poem. Try to find another poem that could be described this way. Then write a definition to explain what Romantic poetry is and a paragraph to explain why 'To a Skylark' is one such example.

or

Focus on the list of sounds that you compiled in the Starter exercise and either write a poem on one of these sounds, using one of the poetic forms that you have come across so far, or choose one of the sounds that you liked and another that you disliked. Write a paragraph on each explaining why you like/dislike them and what they make you think of.

Eagles

- To look at how poems which share the same theme can have very different meanings;
- To contrast descriptions of eagles as given by three poets;
- To compare the various points of view;
- To reflect on the wider meanings of poems;
- To prepare a brief talk and deliver it to the class.

1 Starter

 With your partner, write a list of as many words as you can that you would associate with eagles. Think about what you know about them. Where do eagles live and what sort of life do they lead? Consider also the way that humans have used eagles as emblems. What kinds of things have these emblems represented?

 When you have completed your list, read the words to the rest of the class. Compile a bank of words you would use to describe these birds.

FACT FILE

Alfred, Lord Tennyson was born in 1809, the son of a vicar. His home life, however, was troubled. He published his first poems when he was 21, two of which were his famous 'Kraken' poem and 'Ode to Memory'. It cost him eleven pounds to publish them but, sadly, few copies were sold. Although Tennyson left Cambridge without completing his degree, he continued to write poetry – encouraged by his friends – and went on to produce some of the finest poems in the English literary heritage.

The Eagle

He clasps the crag with crooked hands;
Close to the sun in lonely lands,
Ring'd with the azure world, he stands.

The wrinkled sea beneath him crawls;
He watches from his mountain walls,
And like a thunderbolt he falls.

Alfred, Lord Tennyson

2 Introduction

With a partner, discuss the eagle in Tennyson's poem. What features has he described?

Now try to imagine what it is like to stand high on the cliffs, almost inside the clouds. An eagle has acute eyesight. Copy the star diagram below into your book and think of as many things as you can that an eagle might see when it is perched on the cliff.

prey

eagle on cliff

mountain top

In the first line of the poem, Tennyson has repeated the same letter at the beginning of several words. This technique is called **alliteration**. It can help to draw the reader's attention to what the poet is saying by giving particular emphasis to the words.

3 Development

In spite of the shortness of the poem, Tennyson has given a detailed account of the eagle's surroundings. Write a paragraph to describe:

everything you know about the place in which the eagle lives;

everything you know about the eagle itself and the way it moves. Why might it fall like a 'thunderbolt'?

or

Think about why poets might want to write about eagles. Now make a list of the most important features of eagles you might use in a poem, using any of the poetic forms you have covered so far.

Answer the following questions to explain how Tennyson's use of alliteration helps to make the opening of this poem more powerful.

- Tennyson has used alliteration in the first line of the poem. Which words has he used? Copy them out.

- What does this line draw our attention to? What is the first image of the eagle that springs to mind?

- Talk with your partner to decide whether you think this is an effective beginning. What effect does the alliteration have?

FACT FILE

David Herbert Lawrence was born in Eastwood in Nottinghamshire. His father was a coal miner and his mother a teacher. He won a scholarship to Nottingham High School then went on to Nottingham University. Lawrence wrote his first poems when he was 19. He writes on themes of love, animals and landscapes, mostly in free verse but also in dialect. He also wrote short stories and essays but is mainly known for his novels.

From: Eagle in New Mexico

Sun-breaster,
Staring two ways at once, to right and left;
Masked-one
Dark-visaged
Sickle-masked
With iron between your two eyes;
You feather-gloved
To the feet;
Foot-fierce;
Erect one;
The god-thrust entering you steadily from below.

You never look at the sun with your two eyes.
Only the inner eye of your scorched broad breast
Looks straight at the sun.

You are dark
Except scorch-pale-breasted;
And dark cleaves down and weapon-hard downward curving
At your scorched breast,
Like a sword of Damocles,
Beaked eagle.

You've dipped it in blood so many times
That dark face-weapon, to temper it well,
Blood-thirsty bird…

D. H. Lawrence

(Note: The legend of the sword of Damocles refers to a sword suspended from above by a single thread under which Damocles dined – any second his life could have ended.)

Introduction

In this extract, D. H. Lawrence describes the appearance of an eagle in fine detail. Discuss the following questions in your group, preparing to feed your answers back to the class.

- What does he tell us about the eagle's eyes?
- What has the poet observed about the eagle's face?
- Why might an eagle be described as 'Foot-fierce'?
- Why is the eagle's 'weapon-hard' beak like a sword of Damocles?
- The eagle is considered to be a very strong bird. What is the source of its power?
- Two other forces have an effect upon the eagle in this poem: the sun, with its life-giving and energising properties, affects the eagle; and 'God', seen as the ultimate source of power in many cultures, touches the eagle too. Which parts of the poem refer to these sources of strength?

- Lawrence has used a lot of combined images in this poem. Look at the words below and, using a dictionary and a thesaurus, see if you can write a sentence to describe the imagery each of them brings to mind.

face-weapon   dark-visaged
scorch-pale-breasted   sickle-masked
god-thrust   foot-fierce

 Development

 Reread both poems. Do the eagles in Tennyson's and Lawrence's poems have anything in common, or have the poets emphasised different features?

Copy out this table and fill it in to help you develop your ideas.

Using the information you have compiled, write three paragraphs on the similarities between the two poems, the differences between them, and which you enjoyed most and why.

	Tennyson	Lawrence
Language used		
How is the eagle described?		
What is the poet saying about the eagle?		
Mood of the poem		

The following poem is by Matthew Sweeney. He weaves a story around an event, which tells us something about the eagles but gives a great deal more away about his father and his own country.

FACT FILE

Matthew Sweeney was born in Co. Donegal, Ireland but moved to England in 1973. He studied German and English at the North London Polytechnic and the University of Freiburg. He now works as a professional writer and has published many poems on varying themes for both adults and children. He is also an anthologist and has written a novel for children.

The Eagle

My father is writing in Irish.
The English language, with all its facts
will not do. It is too modern.
It is good for plane-crashes, for unemployment,
but not for the unexplained return
of the eagle to Donegal.

He describes the settled pair
in their eyrie on the not-so-high mountain.
He uses an archaic Irish
to describe what used to be, what is again,
though hungers are reluctant
to agree on what will be.

He's coined a new word
for vigilantes who keep a camera watch
on the foothills. He joins them
when he's not writing, and when he is.
He writes about giant eggs,
about a whole new strain.

He brings in folklore
and folk-prophecy. He brings in the date
when the last golden eagle
was glimpsed there. The research is new
and dodgy, but the praise
is as old as the eagle.

Matthew Sweeney

1 Introduction

In your groups, talk about and make notes on the following questions.

- Why does the poet's father want to write in Irish rather than in English? In what special way might the two languages be different? How might writing in Irish be more suitable for this subject?

- Which two lines in the poem suggest the father gains pleasure from using the Irish language?

- How do you think the poet's father feels about the eagles' return to Ireland? Which parts of the poem allowed you to work this out?
- What do you think is meant by the terms 'folklore' and 'folk-prophecy'?
- The research produced by the father is 'new and dodgy'. What does this tell you about the father's account of the eagles' return?
- Is the poet proud of his father, or do you feel he is critical of his father's ways? If there are differences of opinion, try to work out which parts of the poem support a particular point of view.

 Development

Matthew Sweeney's poem is about an eagle. We know this from the title, but there are also other messages in the poem. Using the notes you have made, answer the following questions. Write a paragraph on each.

- Does he describe the eagle in any great detail?
- What can you say about his feelings for his father?
- What does he say about the Irish and English languages?

 Plenary

Copy the following chart into your book. Match the descriptions of the eagles to the correct poem from the three you have read to show how each has a different theme and point of view.

Eagle as:	Poem
Fearsome	
A curiosity	
A source of power and strength	
A part of folklore	
A creature to be identified with	
A symbol	
An unpredictable creature	
A part of nature	

 Homework

Using the library or the internet, find out what you can about eagles. Prepare a three-minute talk to give to the class on the aspect of them you find most interesting. For example, you might talk about the way they have been used as a symbol over the ages, or about their natural habitat.

Love

- To learn about ballads and respond to the poem as an 'active' audience;
- To think about how the entertainment value of a poem is enhanced through performance;
- To study the pictorial imagery and tuneful quality of poetry;
- To see how tension is built up through language and structure;
- To study the poetic form of a sonnet;
- To create a sonnet of your own.

A **ballad** is a poem that tells a story, often a dramatic one, full of adventure, love, death or war. The earliest ballads were folk tales, often set to music and performed in front of audiences who were encouraged to join in by repeating the lines or chanting the choruses. Many ballads were never written down, but instead were passed on by word of mouth.

In the ballad 'The Highwayman', by Alfred Noyes, tension is built up as the story progresses. The poem begins as the highwayman comes riding onto the page, bringing drama into our minds from another century.

1 Starter

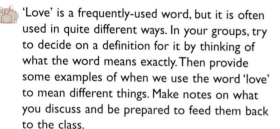

'Love' is a frequently-used word, but it is often used in quite different ways. In your groups, try to decide on a definition for it by thinking of what the word means exactly. Then provide some examples of when we use the word 'love' to mean different things. Make notes on what you discuss and be prepared to feed them back to the class.

FACT FILE

Alfred Noyes was born in 1880 in Wolverhampton and educated in Wales and Oxford. He wrote poems, novels and plays. 'The Highwayman' has become a popular ballad in the English literary heritage.

The Highwayman

PART ONE

The wind was a torrent of darkness among the gusty trees,
The moon was a ghostly galleon tossed upon cloudy seas,
The road was a ribbon of moonlight, over the purple moor,
And the highwayman came riding –
Riding – riding –
The highwayman came riding, up to the old inn-door.

He'd a French cocked-hat on his forehead, a bunch of lace at his chin,
A coat of the claret velvet, and breeches of brown doe-skin:
They fitted with never a wrinkle: his boots were up to the thigh
And he rode with a jewelled twinkle,
His pistol butts a-twinkle,
His rapier hilt a-twinkle, under the jewelled sky.

Over the cobbles he clattered and clashed in the dark inn-yard,
And he tapped with his whip on the shutters, but all was locked and barred.
He whistled a tune to the window, and who should be waiting there
But the landlord's black-eyed daughter,
Bess, the landlord's daughter,
Plaiting a dark red love-knot into her long black hair.

And dark in the dark old inn-yard a stable-wicket creaked
Where Tim the ostler listened; his face was white and peaked;
His eyes were hollows of madness, his hair like mouldy hay,
But he loved the landlord's daughter,
The landlord's red-lipped daughter,
Dumb as a dog he listened, and he heard the robber say –

"One kiss, my bonny sweetheart, I'm after a prize to-night,
But I shall be back with the yellow gold before the morning light;
Yet, if they press me sharply, and harry me through the day,
Then look for me by moonlight,
Watch for me by moonlight,
I'll come to thee by moonlight, though hell should bar the way."

He rose upright in the stirrups; he scarce could reach her hand,
But she loosened her hair i' the casement! His face burnt like a brand
As the black cascade of perfume came tumbling over his breast;
And he kissed its waves in the moonlight,
(Oh, sweet black waves in the moonlight!)
Then he tugged at his reins in the moonlight, and galloped away to the west.

PART TWO

He did not come in the dawning; he did not come at noon;
And out o' the tawny sunset, before the rise o' the moon,
When the road was a gypsy's ribbon, looping the purple moor,
A red-coat troop came marching –
Marching – marching –
King George's men came marching, up to the old inn-door.

They said no word to the landlord, they drank his ale instead,
But they gagged his daughter and bound her to the foot of her narrow bed.
Two of them knelt at her casement, with muskets at their side!
There was death at every window;
And hell at one dark window;
For Bess could see, through the casement, the road that *he* would ride.

They had tied her up to attention, with many a sniggering jest;
They bound a musket beside her, with the barrel beneath her breast!
"Now keep good watch!" and they kissed her.
She heard the dead man say –
Look for me by moonlight;
Watch for me by moonlight;
I'll come to thee by moonlight, though hell should bar the way!

She twisted her hands behind her; but all the knots held good!
She writhed her hands till her fingers were wet with sweat or blood!
They stretched and stained in the darkness, and the hours crawled by like years,
Till, now, on the stroke of midnight,
Cold, on the stroke of midnight,
The tip of one finger touched it! The trigger at least was hers!

The tip of one finger touched it; she strove no more for the rest.
Up, she stood up to attention, with the barrel beneath her breast.
She would not risk their hearing; she would not strive again;
For the road lay bare in the moonlight;
Blank and bare in the moonlight;
And the blood of her veins in the moonlight throbbed to her love's refrain.

Tlot-tlot; tlot-tlot! Had they heard it? The horse-hoofs ringing clear;
Tlot-tlot, tlot-tlot, in the distance! Were they deaf that they did not hear?
Down the ribbon of moonlight, over the brow of the hill,
The highwayman came riding,
Riding, riding!
The red-coats looked to their priming! She stood up straight and still!

Tlot-tlot, in the frosty silence! *Tlot-tlot,* in the echoing night!
Nearer he came and nearer. Her face was like a light.
Her eyes grew wide for a moment; she drew one last deep breath,
Then her finger moved in the moonlight,
Her musket shattered the moonlight,
Shattered her breast in the moonlight and warned him – with her death.

He turned; he spurred to the west; he did not know who stood
Bowed with her head o'er the musket, drenched with her own red blood!
Not till the dawn he heard it, his face grew grey to hear
How Bess, the landlord's daughter,
The landlord's black-eyed daughter,
Had watched for her love in the moonlight, and died in the darkness there.

Back, he spurred like a madman, shrieking a curse to the sky,
With the white road smoking behind him and his rapier brandished high!
Blood-red were his spurs i' the golden noon;
wine-red was his velvet coat,
When they shot him down on the highway,
Down like a dog on the highway,
And he lay in his blood on the highway, with the bunch of lace at his throat.

And still of a winter's night, they say, when the wind is in the trees,
When the moon is a ghostly galleon tossed upon cloudy seas,
When the road is a ribbon of moonlight over the purple moor,
A highwayman comes riding –
Riding – riding –
A highwayman comes riding, up to the old inn-door.

*Over the cobbles he clatters and clangs in the dark
inn-yard;
And he taps with his whip on the shutters, but all is
locked and barred;
He whistles a tune to the window, and who should be
waiting there
But the landlord's black-eyed daughter,
Bess, the landlord's daughter,
Plaiting a dark red love-knot into her long black hair.*

Alfred Noyes

3 Development

Noyes uses three poetic techniques to help create the rhythm and musical quality of the poem.

*Listen to the sound effect achieved in the line: 'Over the cobbles he clattered and clashed…' When sounds are repeated like this for emphasis, it is known as **alliteration**. Here, we can almost hear the sound of the horse's hooves as it clatters across the cobbles.*

*Sound effects like **onomatopoeia** happen when a word sounds like a noise that is being made, for example the buzz of a bee. It is used in 'The Highwayman' when we hear the 'Tlot-tlot' of the horse's hooves. This also creates the rhythm of the poem.*

*Other words are also repeated regularly in the poem too, using what is called a chorus or **refrain**. This is done to emphasise important parts of the story and to create a tuneful and musical effect as the tale unfolds.*

2 Introduction

 Reread the poem. Then, in your pairs, discuss the following questions to show your understanding of the story.

- What was the highwayman's plan?
- Who is listening and what is he going to do?
- What happens when 'King George's men' arrive at the inn in Part II of the poem?
- How does Bess warn her lover?
- When the highwayman finds out what has happened, what does he do?
- What do you think he is hoping he can do against 'King George's men'? How would you describe his actions?
- Look at the last two stanzas. How do we know that this is a different time from the rest of the poem? When is it?

 With your partner, find all the references to the three characters described in Part I of 'The Highwayman'. Who are they? Draw a portrait for each and surround it with adjectives describing their character – including phrases from the poem.

The narrative, or story, in the poem unfolds quickly. Each stanza moves the story on to keep the reader interested. Look how the story unfolds as the lines continue. Select six or seven key episodes from the poem and storyboard these with captions.

 Discuss the following and be prepared to feed back what you find to the class.

- Read Part I of the poem. How many examples of alliteration, onomatopoeia and refrain can you find?
- Repeated sounds and rhythms play very important roles in this poem and add to its atmosphere. Scan the poem for any examples of sounds we can almost hear as we read them. For example, 'He tapped with his whip on the shutters'. Can you find more?
- Work on preparing a single stanza of the poem to perform to the class. Think carefully about how you will create atmosphere by the way you relate the story. Think about volume and tone of voice, emphasis of certain words, pace, and so on.

 The story takes place on a dark and windy, moonlit night. Find two or three lines or phrases that describe the night the highwayman rides in.

The following paragraph openers may help you.

- The phrases… and… tell us what sort of a night it was when the highwayman went to the inn.
- The line… also describes it.
- The atmosphere at the start of the poem is…
- It is suitable for the story because…

Now make notes in answer to these questions.

- Why does Noyes describe the highwayman as riding with 'a jewelled twinkle'?
- In what way is the sky also 'jewelled'?
- How does using the word 'jewelled' to describe both the sky and the highwayman add to the poem's imagery?
- Making comparisons can often create powerful pictures in the mind. A **metaphor** is also a type of comparison, where one thing is being compared with another. Find the words the poet has used to describe the wind, the moon, the road and Bess's hair. For each example, say what they are being compared with and why the comparison is effective.

The second poem in this unit is a sonnet by the great English poet and playwright, William Shakespeare. It speaks of love in a lofty way, using much more **poetic diction**, which means using words that today might seem artificial.

> The **sonnet** is a poem of 14 lines, usually expressing a single idea or sentiment (often love), and with rhymes arranged in a definite scheme. It is written in three quatrains — that is, groups of four lines — followed by a couplet, of two lines. The pattern is abab, cdcd, efef, gg, as you will see below.

FACT FILE

William Shakespeare was born in 1564 in Stratford-upon-Avon, Warwickshire. He married Anne Hathaway in 1582 with whom he had a daughter in 1583, then twins, Hamnet and Judith, in 1585. He is first mentioned as a playwright in 1592 and wrote many famous plays and poems.

Sonnet 17

Who will believe my verse in time to come	(a)
If it were fill'd with your most high deserts?	(b)
Though yet, heaven knows, it is but as a tomb	(a)
Which hides your life and shows not half your parts.	(b)
If I could write the beauty of your eyes	(c)
And in fresh numbers all your graces,	(d)
The age to come would say, 'This poet lies;	(c)
Such heavenly touches ne'er touch'd earthly faces.'	(d)
So should my papers, yellowed with their age,	(e)
Be scorn'd, like old men of less truth than tongue,	(f)
And your true rights be term'd a poet's rage	(e)
And stretched metre of an antique song:	(f)
But were some child of yours alive that time,	(g)
You should live twice, – in it and in my rime.	(g)

William Shakespeare

2 Development

Select at least three of the words below that might best describe this sonnet:

clever   sad   funny   romantic   sentimental
maudlin   witty   ironic

Look up any difficult words in a dictionary and write a paragraph on each of the words you have chosen, explaining why you have made your particular choices.

The rhyme scheme of the sonnet is abab, cdcd, efef, gg. Some of the words almost rhyme but don't quite. These are known as loose rhymes. Write down the last word of each of the lines. Notice the words that rhyme fully and those that don't. In what ways might the loose rhymes work just as well in a different way?

3 Plenary

Perform 'The Highwayman' as a group or class. Discuss what makes this poem effective and memorable.

Why might reciting it be more of an experience than reciting something else?

Explain the difference between a sonnet and a ballad. What are the main differences between the two poems you have studied?

4 Homework

Write 14 lines about someone or something about which you feel strongly. (This could be a relative, friend, a pet, possession or place.) When you have written your sonnet, ask someone else to read it and invite comments. Once you are happy with what you have written, write it out neatly.

or

Using the library or internet, see if you can find examples of other ballads. Ask older relatives if they know of any traditional songs or ballads from where they live or from other parts of world.

1 Introduction

As a class, read the poem aloud. Then, in your groups, make notes on the following questions.

- What do you think the relationship is between Shakespeare and the person about whom he is writing? Find specific words and lines in the poem to justify what you say.

- What images do you have of the person in the poem? Why do you think beauty is often hard to describe?

- What is meant by 'your most high deserts' and what Shakespeare calls a 'stretched metre of an antique song'?

- Does he feel he can never really capture what he wants to say in his poem? If so, why does he think this way?

- Can you find two lines in the poem that suggest his readers might think he exaggerates? Compare your answers with those of another group. Are they in any way similar?

- In the final couplet, Shakespeare mentions a child. What does he mean when he says that the person he loves could 'live twice'?

Loss

- To consider the subject of loss in a variety of ways, and examine the forms poets have used to express it;
- To understand how a villanelle is created;
- To learn about 'metaphysical' poetry;
- To learn about rap;
- To reinforce the meaning of loose rhyme;
- To learn about suffixes and prefixes.

1 Starter

Coming to terms with loss and accepting that people are never coming back is a subject that appears frequently in books, on television and in films. In your groups, try to think of five stories on these themes and decide why they are so popular.

FACT FILE

Dylan Thomas was born in Swansea in 1914 and for a time, after he left school, worked for a Swansea newspaper. Later he went to live in London and reviewed thrillers for newspapers. As well as writing poetry and short stories, he also wrote for the radio and recited poetry with immense skill. Thomas drank heavily and died in the USA in 1953, aged 39. His early death is thought to have been hastened by his excessive drinking.

Do Not Go Gentle Into That Good Night

Do not go gentle into that good night,
Old age should burn and rave at close of day;
Rage, rage against the dying of the light.

Though wise men at their end know dark is right,
Because their words had forked no lightning they
Do not go gentle into that good night,

Good men, the last wave by, crying how bright
Their frail deeds might have danced in a green bay,
Rage, rage against the dying of the light.

Wild men who caught and sang the sun in flight,
And learn, too late, they grieved it on its way,
Do not go gentle into that good night.

Grave men, near death, who see with blinding sight
Blind eyes could blaze like meteors and be gay,
Rage, rage against the dying of the light.

And you, my father, there on the sad height,
Curse, bless, me now with your fierce tears, I pray.
Do not go gentle into that good night.
Rage, rage against the dying of the light.

Dylan Thomas

2 Introduction

In your groups, read the poem again and work through the questions below, making notes on your answers. Be prepared to talk with the rest of the class about what you find.

■ Who are all the people mentioned in the poem?

■ What is Thomas saying about how all people should approach death?

■ What is the effect of not mentioning his own father until the final stanza?

■ When Thomas says 'their words had forked no lightning', what do you think he means?

■ The 'dying of the light' is an example of Thomas personifying the light by making it into a living thing that dies. In what other ways might death be personified?

> Notice how Thomas uses personification when he creates images, giving a life force to ideas and things. For instance, 'frail deeds' dance 'in a green bay'. Of course deeds cannot really dance, but through personification they can.

■ Pick out two other reasons from the poem why you should 'not go gentle'. What do you think each of them means?

■ Do you agree with Thomas's view? Are there any situations when you think that a different view would be appropriate?

Still paying close attention to the poem, copy the chart below into your books. Find the lines from the poem to help you answer the questions.

Question	Lines from the poem to back up your view	Answer
What does Thomas mean when he says that men near death 'see with blinding sight' and that even blind eyes might 'blaze like meteors'?		
Why do you think Thomas asks his father to both bless and curse him with 'fierce tears'?		
What sort of atmosphere does Thomas create in the poem? Choose some words from the following list: tense happy sad guilty miserable jubilant grave exciting		
What is the effect of repetition in the poem? Why is it effective? How does it help us to understand Thomas's feelings?		

Development

Writing a villanelle

Dylan Thomas's poem, 'Do Not Go Gentle Into That Good Night', is written in the form of a villanelle. A villanelle provides the drama for the poem by emphasising particular lines.

As a class, recite the poem, emphasising the repeated lines. Discuss why doing this is effective.

The villanelle has 19 lines, arranged in six stanzas. The first five stanzas have just three lines each. The last stanza has four. Look at Dylan Thomas's poem and see how the stanzas are organised.

Now look at the first and third line of the first stanza. You will see that they have been repeated alternately as the last lines of the second to the fifth stanza before both being used to finish the sixth stanza.

Stanza 1

(line 1) Do not go gentle into that good night,

(line 3) Rage, rage against the dying of the light.

Stanza 2

(line 3) Do not go gentle into that good night.

Stanza 3

(line 3) Rage, rage against the dying of the light,

Stanza 4

(line 3) Do not go gentle into that good night.

Stanza 5

(line 3) Rage, rage against the dying of the light.

Stanza 6

(line 3) Do not go gentle into that good night.

(line 4) Rage, rage against the dying of the light.

The other lines in each stanza must convey the 'thought' and content of the poem, whilst the main concern, to rage and not go gently into death, are drummed out in a regular beat to the final line.

Write a villanelle of your own. You may want to use the lines provided below by copying them into your book, or else write some of your own following the pattern. Think about the main things you are going to say that will fill the body of the poem. This is known as the **content**.

Do not buy me strawberries, mother.

....

Strawberries bring me out in spots.

....
....

Do not buy me strawberries mother.

....
....

Strawberries bring me out in spots.

....
....

Do not buy me strawberries, mother.

....
....

Strawberries bring me out in spots.

....
....

Do not buy me strawberries, mother.

Strawberries bring me out in spots.

FACT FILE

Grace Nichols was born in 1950 in the South American country of Guyana and grew up there. She became a teacher and then a newspaper reporter. Later she began to write poetry. Now living in Britain, she has published many books for children and adults.

This second poem is also about death. Grace Nichols is concerned about the 'sort' of death a 'fat black woman' wants and feels is right for her when she has to die.

Tropical Death

The fat black woman want
a brilliant tropical death
not a cold sojourn
in some North Europe far/forlorn

The fat black woman want
some heat/hibiscus at her feet
blue sea dress
to wrap her neat

The fat black woman want
some bawl
no quiet jerk tear wiping
a polite hearse withdrawal

The fat black woman want
all her dead rights
first night
third night
nine night
all the sleepless droning
red-eyed wake nights

In the heart
of her mother's sweetbreast
In the shade
of the sun leaf's cool bless
In the bloom
of her people's bloodrest

the fat black woman want
a brilliant tropical death yes

Grace Nichols

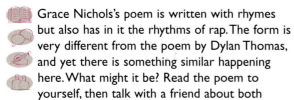

1 Introduction

Grace Nichols's poem is written with rhymes but also has in it the rhythms of rap. The form is very different from the poem by Dylan Thomas, and yet there is something similar happening here. What might it be? Read the poem to yourself, then talk with a friend about both poems and think about how they are spoken.

Rap is exactly what it says, a sharp rapping sound with a pronounced beat to which the words are recited. As a class, read the poem, stressing the rap in the words.

Make notes about the effect of combining the words 'far/forlorn' when the woman talks about the country she does not want to die in. Select some words from the poem to add to the chart below to contrast her feelings about how and where she wants to die.

Want	Not want
a brilliant tropical death	a cold sojourn in North Europe

2 Development

What is the mood or atmosphere of the poem? Write in prose what the poet is saying. Search the stanzas for lines to help you support your answer. The sentence openers below may help.

- The 'fat black woman' is asking…
- The two places she talks about are contrasted by the lines…
- Her love of the tropical climate is shown by the words…
- She feels that 'North Europe far/forlorn' is… and that she will be better…
- 'In the bloom of her people's bloodrest.' There they will… with 'red-eyed wake nights.'

FACT FILE

Roger McGough was born in Liverpool and went to Hull University. He was one of the Liverpool Poets, together with Brian Patten and Adrian Henri, who gave a special boost to poetry – as the Beatles had done to music. He has written many books for both adults and children.

The third poem, 'Survivor', combines a serious tone with a humorous one to brilliant effect.

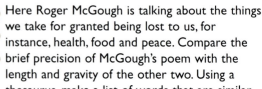

Survivor

Everyday
I think about dying.
About disease, starvation,
violence, terrorism, war,
the end of the world.

It helps
keep my mind off things.

Roger McGough

1 Introduction

Here Roger McGough is talking about the things we take for granted being lost to us, for instance, health, food and peace. Compare the brief precision of McGough's poem with the length and gravity of the other two. Using a thesaurus, make a list of words that are similar to the word 'survivor' and say how they might apply to the poem.

Bearing in mind that Roger McGough is a modern poet living in the UK, where is it most likely that he will come across the things that he mentions in his poem?

What kinds of things might he need to take his mind off?

2 Development

In what ways is the poem both serious and funny? With a partner, decide why this might be and then write three paragraphs on:

- why the poem is humorous;

- why the poem has a serious side;

- what you think Roger McGough is trying to say;

- things we take for granted that are not available to many people in other parts of the world.

FACT FILE

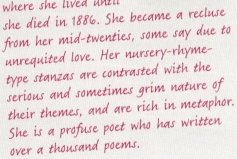

Emily Dickinson was born in 1830 in Amherst, Massachusetts where she lived until she died in 1886. She became a recluse from her mid-twenties, some say due to unrequited love. Her nursery-rhyme-type stanzas are contrasted with the serious and sometimes grim nature of their themes, and are rich in metaphor. She is a profuse poet who has written over a thousand poems.

The fourth poem by Emily Dickinson, like much of her work, is strange and mysterious. Read the poem to yourself.

I Felt a Funeral In My Brain

I felt a funeral in my brain,
And mourners, to and fro,
Kept treading, treading, till it seemed
That sense was breaking through.

And when they all were seated,
A service like a drum
Kept beating, beating, till I thought
My mind was going numb.

And then I heard them lift a box,
And creak across my soul
With those same boots of lead, again
Then space began to toll

As all the heavens were a bell,
And being but an ear,
And I and silence some strange race,
Wrecked, solitary, here.

And then a Plank in Reason, broke,
And I dropped down, and down –
And hit a World, at every plunge,
And Finished knowing – then –

Emily Dickinson

This poem is written in five, four-line stanzas. Note the second and fourth lines of the first stanza, which end with 'fro' and 'through'. This is known as a **loose rhyme** because the words almost but do not quite rhyme. This technique is often used by poets since it can frequently go unnoticed if done cleverly.

A poem like this that uses abstract ideas — that is, ideas that are general and without definate truths, like thoughts about souls, ghosts, or visions — is called a **metaphysical** poem. Metaphysical poems were often written in the seventeenth century when people were very religious and strongly believed in the supernatural. The roots of the word 'metaphysical' come from Greek and Latin, the Greek word 'meta' generally meaning after or beyond, and 'physical' built up from the Latin words 'physica' and the Greek 'phusike' meaning knowledge of nature. So you can see how the word has been created from the old languages to mean 'after or beyond knowledge of nature'.

Introduction

Look up the following words in a thesaurus or dictionary and make a list of synonyms.

numb   mourners   lead   wrecked   solitary
creak   beat(ing)

Look at the word lists you have created. What can you say about:

- the atmosphere in the poem?
- the narrative the poet recounts of what she imagines inside her brain?
- what you think the poet is trying to say?

Development

With a partner, discuss the following questions and make notes on your ideas.

- Who or what do you think the 'mourners' in the poet's brain are?
- The mourners keep 'treading, treading' and the service keeps 'beating, beating'. What is the effect of this repetition?
- What do you think is in the box that creaks across Dickinson's soul? What is she hearing when she says that her being is just 'an ear'?
- Dickinson talks of 'I and silence' being 'some strange race' — that is, wrecked and solitary. What might she be trying to say through these mysterious words?
- Reread the last stanza of Dickinson's poem. What do you think she might mean when she says 'a Plank in Reason' broke, and she dropped down somewhere?
- What could she mean by 'Finished knowing –'? Knowing what?

Plenary

The poets have written about death in four different ways. How do they differ?

What is meant by a villanelle and why might this form be right for what Dylan Thomas is saying?

What do you understand by the word 'metaphysical'? In what ways can 'I Felt a Funeral In My Brain' be descibed as a metaphysical poem?

Homework

Write a poem of your own about something metaphysical — perhaps a supernatural event or something you dreamed.

or

Read the three poems again (as well as the notes you have made). Say what it is that each poet is most concerned about and how they have tried to come to terms with this through their poem.

Remembering

AIMS

- To learn how to elicit meaning from given lines in a poem;
- To develop confidence in considering the wider meanings of words;
- To think about the effect of form upon meaning;
- To reinforce understanding of how rhyme schemes work;
- To consider poetic form and style when writing about memories.

Starter

 The landscape of our lives is constantly changing. Try to remember your early childhood. You may remember a house or building you once knew or lived in. What is your earliest memory? Why do think you can remember it?

 Write the heading 'Memorabilia' in your books. List five things you once owned and really liked but no longer have. Opposite each, write down what you think about when you remember them. An example has been done for you.

What I no longer have	What I remember most
Red socks with toes	Wore holes in them and had to throw them out.

FACT FILE

William Butler Yeats was born in London in 1865 but grew up in Ireland where he became one of Ireland's most famous poets. He was deeply interested in philosophy and religion, history, mystery and magic, which are important themes in his work. Yeats was awarded The Nobel Prize for Literature in 1923. He died in 1939.

The first poem in this unit reflects on the role that memory plays as people grow old.

When You Are Old

When you are old and gray and full of sleep,
And nodding by the fire, take down this book,
And slowly read, and dream of the soft look
Your eyes had once, and of their shadows deep;

How many loved your moments of glad grace,
And loved your beauty with love false or true;
But one man loved the pilgrim soul in you,
And loved the sorrows of your changing face.

And bending down beside the glowing bars
Murmur, a little sadly, how love fled
And placed upon the mountains overhead
And hid his face amid a crown of stars.

W. B. Yeats

Introduction

  In groups, discuss the following questions and make notes on your answers.

- The poet says the person in this poem has a 'soft look' in her eyes and 'glad grace' that he wants her to remember when the poem is read later in life. Who might he be addressing?

- What else does he want her to remember when she is 'old and gray'?

- The speaker says, '… one man loved the pilgrim soul in you'. What does he mean by 'the pilgrim soul'? Why have the words 'pilgrim' and 'soul' been linked in the poem? Use a dictionary to help you.

- What is the relationship between the narrator (the person who speaks in the poem) and the subject (the person who is being spoken about)? What evidence can you find in the poem to support what you say?

- What might have happened to the bond they once had? With reference to the poem, say how you have formed your opinion.

Development

 One of the words you might use to describe this poem is 'reflective', since the speaker is thinking about his relationship with the subject and wondering how things will be remembered in later life. Choose three words from the following to suggest its mood:

sad   romantic   nostalgic   angry   irritable   wistful   melancholy   loving

Write one sentence for each of the words you have chosen, explaining why you think each word is suitable for describing the poem. Wherever possible, use quotations from the poem to support your views.

  Look at the words at the ends of the lines listed below. Notice how each new rhyming word has the next letter of the alphabet beside it. This shows that a new rhyming sound has come into the poem. This allows you to see the poem's rhyming pattern.

Stanza 1	Stanza 2	Stanza 3
sleep (a)	grace (c)	bars (e)
book (b)	true (d)	fled (f)
look (b)	you (d)	overhead (f)
deep (a)	face (c)	stars (e)

Choose four words from the list and include them in a paragraph about someone you are close to growing older. Say how you might feel about this.

Of 'In the attic', the second poem in this unit, Andrew Motion says: 'I wrote this poem when I was twenty years old, and (unusually) I wrote it very quickly. I wanted to capture the ghostly mixture of presence and absence that a dead person's clothes have, and to suggest that the same mixture survives in our memories of the person themselves.'

In the attic

Even though we know now
your clothes will never
be needed, we keep them,
upstairs in a locked trunk.

Sometimes I kneel there,
touching them, trying to relive
time you wore them, to remember
the actual shape of arm and wrist.

My hands push down between
hollow, invisible sleeves,
hesitate, then take hold
and lift:

a green holiday; a red christening;
all your finished lives
fading through dark summers,
entering my head as dust.

Andrew Motion

 ## Introduction

 Grief can be a difficult emotion to write or talk about. In this poem, the poet shares with us some very intimate aspects of grief. He does not, however, write about his feelings directly but invites us into a scene in which we too can experience the pain of his loss.

In groups, discuss the following questions and make notes on your answers.

- Old clothes aren't usually valuable. Why might they be locked in a trunk? Why is it significant that the trunk is locked?

- The sleeves are 'hollow' and 'invisible'. Why do you think the poet has chosen these words?

- Why might the poet hesitate before taking hold of the sleeves? Why is he lifting up the clothes?

- Who do you think the narrator is? What do you think their relationship was with the deceased person?

- In the first line of the poem, the pronoun 'we' is used. What does this tell us about who is grieving?

- What memories return to the speaker when he is in the attic?

- What moments of sadness has the poem captured?

2 Development

In both 'When You Are Old' and 'In the attic', there is a suggestion of a close and loving relationship between the narrator and the subject of the poem. Using the notes you have made on both poems, compare and contrast them, making sure that you have covered the following points.

- The narrators' relationship with the subject of the poem – in what ways are they similar and in what ways are they different?
- The things that they remember.
- How you feel about both the poems and why.

FACT FILE

Elaine Feinstein is a poet, novelist and playwright. In 1980 she was made a Fellow of the Royal Society of Literature. She was born in Bootle, Lancashire, and was educated at Newnham College, Cambridge. She writes in a clear direct style on themes of love, family, friends and music with a strong emotional atmosphere, and has been translated into 14 languages.

Of 'Dad' Elaine Feinstein says: 'I admired my father all through my childhood, seeing even his faults as virtues, particularly his reckless extravagance and obstinacy. When he came to live with my husband and three sons, I discovered he was hard to cope with, and I didn't behave well, which made his death all the harder to bear. This poem came out of that grief, and helped to resolve my guilt.'

Dad

Your old hat hurts me, and those black
fat raisins you liked to press into
my palm from your soft heavy hand.
I see you staggering back up the path
with sacks of potatoes from some local farm,
fresh eggs, flowers. Every day I grieve

for your great heart broken and you gone.
You loved to watch the trees. This year
you did not see their Spring.
The sky was freezing over the fen
as on that somewhere secretly appointed day
you beached: cold, white-faced, shivering.

What happened, old bull, my loyal
hoarse-voiced warrior? The hammer
blow that stopped you in your track
and brought you to a hospital monitor
could not destroy your courage
to the end you were
uncowed and unconcerned with pleasing anyone.

I think of you now as once again safely
at my mother's side, the earth as
chosen as a bed, and feel most sorrow for
all that was gentle in
my childhood buried there
already forfeit, now forever lost.

Elaine Feinstein

Introduction

Throughout her poem, Elaine Feinstein uses language to create a sense of her father's physical presence. He liked to 'press' raisins into her hand; he has a 'great' heart; she sees him 'staggering back up the path/with sacks of potatoes'; he watches the trees; and there is the physical presence of the sky 'freezing over the fen', the hospital, and then the earth in which he is finally laid.

Search for the words and phrases in the poem that convey Dad's strength of both body and character. Write them down and discuss their effectiveness.

Reread the poem and look carefully at how the poet sets up a contrast between the warm and positive images of Dad and the negative, cold images of death. Use the star diagrams below to explore how Feinstein's language conveys these ideas to create two very different sets of images. Some of the words have already been added for you.

flowers

positive things

loyal

Development

In your own words, compare the feelings of grief and regret as expressed in 'In the attic' and 'Dad'. Make sure you cover the following points.

■ What each poem is about.
■ How the sense of grief is presented.
■ The memories from each poem.
■ What you know about the people being remembered.

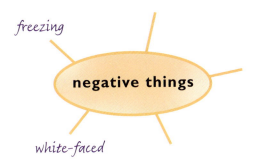

freezing

negative things

white-faced

The fourth poem, 'East Moors', by Gillian Clarke deals with the effects of a changing environment and the way people remember what places were once like, and how they associate them with their own personal thoughts and feelings.

East Moors

FACT FILE

Gillian Clarke was born in 1937 in Cardiff and has lived in Wales for most of her life. She is a broadcaster, freelance writer and lecturer, and has published many highly successful collections of poetry. She edited the Anglo-Welsh Review from 1975–1984, and currently teaches on the MA course in Creative Writing at the University of Glamorgan.

At the end of a bitter April
the cherries flower at last in Penylan.
We notice the white trees and the flash
of sea with two blue islands beyond
the city, where the steelworks used to smoke.

I live in the house I was born in,
am accustomed to the sudden glow
of flame in the night sky, the dark sound
of something heavy dropped, miles off,
the smell of sulphur almost natural.

In Roath and Rumney now, washing strung
down the narrow gardens will stay clean.
Lethargy settles in front rooms and wives
have lined up little jobs for men to do.

A few men stay to see it through. Theirs
the bitterest time as rolling mills
make rubble. Demolition gangs
erase skylines whose hieroglyphs
recorded all our stories.

I am reminded of that Sunday
years ago when we brought the children
to watch two water cooling towers
blown up, recall the appalling void
in the sunlight, like a death.

On this first day of May an icy
rain is blowing through this town,
quieter, cleaner, poorer from today.
The cherries are in flower in Penylan.
Already over East Moors the sky whitens, blind.

Gillian Clarke

1 Introduction

The idea of contrast is an important part of this poem. The landscape of now is contrasted with the landscape of then. Find some lines in the poem to say how Penylan used to be and how it is now. Copy and complete the table in your book.

Penylan then	Penylan now
sudden glow of flame	*demolition gangs*

2 Development

In pairs, discuss the following questions and make notes on your answers.

- Does the narrator seem happy with these changes? How can you tell?

- Why does she describe the demolition of the cooling towers as 'like a death'?

- What effect has the closing of the steelworks had on the lives of the people in the community?

- From the evidence in the poem, what was Penylan like before?

- What does the poet mean when she says that the skylines 'recorded all our stories'?

'East Moors' is unlike the other poems in that although there is a narrator's voice, it doesn't concern a single person but rather an entire community. Using lines from the poem to support your ideas, write a paragraph on each of the following.

- The town as the poet remembers it – what was it like?

- The town as it is now – what has happened to the people and place?

- The ways in which the poet conveys a sense of hopelessness for the town's inhabitants.

3 Plenary

How can writing a poem help you to hold on to memories?

What are the different kinds of remembering in the poems in this unit? Which did you enjoy the most?

4 Homework

Use the poems you have studied to help you write a poem of your own about your memories. Think about a particular person or place that moves you, and try to use contrasting imagery to show how things have changed. Make notes first, then put your notes into order to write your poem.

Words to a Loved One

■ To contrast form and language
and increase understanding of personification;

■ To understand the power of individual words;

■ To reinforce knowledge of imagery;

■ To learn the meaning of 'dirge' and 'lament'.

1 Starter

As a class, talk about different situations when you might have to say goodbye to someone, for instance if they are moving away or leaving school to live a long way off, or even abroad. Why can this be a difficult time where it is important to say the right things? How would you try to keep contacts open?

In 'Away and See', by Carol Ann Duffy, it seems that the narrator is addressing someone they love who is going away. Read the poem to yourself, then try to answer the questions.

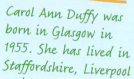

FACT FILE

Carol Ann Duffy was born in Glasgow in 1955. She has lived in Staffordshire, Liverpool and London, and now in Manchester. Graduating in Philosophy from Liverpool University in 1977, she has published several highly successful collections of poetry and won many awards, including an OBE. She has also written plays and an anthology for teenagers.

Away and See

Away and see an ocean suck at a boiled sun
and say to someone things I'd blush even to dream.
Slip off your dress in a high room over the harbour.
Write to me soon.

New fruits sing on the flipside of night in a market
of language, light, a tune from the chapel nearby
stopping you dead, the peach in your palm respiring.
Taste it for me.

Away and see the things that words give a name to, the flight
of syllables, wingspan stretching a noun. Test words
wherever they live; listen and touch, smell, believe.
Spell them with love.

Skedaddle. Somebody chaps at the door at a year's end,
   hopeful.
Away and see who it is. Let in the new, the vivid,
horror and pity, passion, the stranger holding the future.
Ask him his name.

Nothing's the same as anything else. Away and see
for yourself. Walk. Fly. Take a boat till land reappears,
altered forever, ringing its bells, alive. Go on. G'on. Gon.
Away and see.

Carol Ann Duffy

2 Introduction

Discuss the following questions and be prepared to feedback your responses to the class.

- Who do you think the loved one is in this poem?

- What is the tone of the poem? Is the narrator cheerful or unhappy? Support your answer by picking out lines from the poem.

- Duffy's images are sometimes hard to picture, though easier to feel. Look at the following lines and try to write down in prose what the words mean. What image is created for you by these words?
  'New fruits sing on the flipside of night in a market of language'
  'an ocean suck at a boiled sun'
  'the flight/of syllables, wingspan stretching a noun'

- The poem, as its title suggests, is about experiencing different cultures and seeing what happens in them. What things does Duffy propose the loved one should do? Write her suggestions down in your own words.

- What do you think is meant by 'Away and see the things that words give a name to'? How many 'things' might there be?

- In what ways would you 'Test words/wherever they live; listen and touch, smell, believe'?

- List five words you like the sound and meaning of, and five words that you dislike.
  Can you explain why you like the words? Make notes to feedback to the class.

3 Development

Look at the questions below and make notes as you respond. Be prepared to discuss your answers with the class.

- 'Skedaddle' is a **colloquial** word. This means it belongs to ordinary, familiar talk between certain groups of people who know what it means. Look up 'skeddadle' in a dictionary then, using a thesaurus, make a star diagram of words that mean something similar. For instance, another colloquialism for the word 'skedaddle' is 'scarper'. How many more can you find?

- Duffy talks about the ocean as if it were a living thing. How, for instance, can an ocean 'suck at a boiled sun'? The ocean is given human characteristics here – this is called **personification**. Can you can find other examples of this in her poem?

- 'Away and See' is written in free verse, though there is plenty of rhyming going on to carry the poem along. There are, however, hidden rhymes, too. Hidden, or inner rhymes, help give the poem rhythm, for example: 'sun' and 'someone', 'room' and 'soon', 'night' and 'light'. Reread the poem to find them. How many can you spot?

- Duffy often uses words that mean several things at once. The word 'chaps', in the fourth stanza, is playful. What other word might it rhyme with that would fit with the poem? Why is 'chaps' so appropriate here?

Copy the following chart into your book and find
lines in the poem that show the thoughts and feelings
of the narrator.

'Away and See'	Lines from the poem
Have the courage to say what you think. There are all sorts of new things for you to learn about and understand. Remember me wherever you are.	
Don't be afraid of new things or powerful feelings. Dare to confront them.	
Everything will be new for you and different from how other people experience it. Just have courage.	

FACT FILE

Christina Rossetti was born in London in 1830. Although she lived mainly in the city, she wrote mostly about the countryside. The themes of her poems are often sad and she is sometimes thought of as a religious poet. She never married and is most famous for 'Goblin Market', generally considered her masterpiece.

The second poem in this unit, 'A Dirge', is in a very different mood from 'Away and See'. Christina Rossetti's poem is a kind of lament for the dead. She lived when people's lives could be short and early deaths were much more common.

A Dirge

Why were you born when the snow was falling?
You should have come to the cuckoo's calling,
Or when grapes are green in the cluster,
Or at least when lithe swallows muster
For their far off flying
From summer dying.

Why did you die when the lambs were cropping?
You should have died at the apples' dropping,
When the grasshopper comes to trouble,
And the wheat-fields are sodden stubble,
And all winds go sighing
For sweet things dying.

Christina Rossetti

1 Introduction

Work in your groups to answer the questions below, making notes on your answers.

From the following words, make two lists to show which best describe the mood or atmosphere of 'A Dirge' and 'Away and See':

happy   content   solemn   grey   positive
excited   distressed   loving   angry   talkative
comforting   miserable   negative   burdensome
cheerful   glad   worried

2 Development

Talk with a partner about Rossetti's poem. What is her main message? What does she say about the seasons? Select some lines from the poem to support your answer. What does the line 'You should have come to the cuckoo's calling' suggest?

Rossetti's poem is written in rhyming couplets, whilst 'Away and See' is in free verse. In what ways might each form be appropriate for what the poem is saying? Use the following paragraph openers to help with your answers.

- The sobbing effect in the dirge is better achieved by… because…
- The free verse form of 'Away and See' allows the poet to…
- The effect of the child's death is emphasised at the end of each stanza by the word…
- The speaker, or narrator, in the Rossetti poem can hear the death of the child in…
- This is contrasted by the birdsong that comes in…
- Death amongst younger people was more common in Rossetti's time because…
- 'Away and See' celebrates the modern times of health, travel and plenty in the lines…

Duffy has used personification in her poem. Think of ways you might personify the following states yourself:

- loneliness   ■ hatred   ■ joy   ■ fear

For example, loneliness might be personified by 'a tearful emptiness'.

3 Plenary

What is meant by an 'inner rhyme' in poetry? What special role it can play in creating a poem? What do you understand by the word 'lament'? Is this the same as a 'dirge'? Use a dictionary to help you answer.

Choose a line you have liked from each poem and be ready to say why you have enjoyed them.

Look at the words at the end of 'Away and See'. How do they help to give the feeling of someone disappearing?

4 Homework

Copy the star diagram below into your book and complete it with the things you would like to see and experience, including countries and activities. Perhaps one day you would like to go paragliding, or see Stonehenge or the pyramids? Choose three of the things that you have added to your diagram and write a paragraph on each, describing them as you imagine them to be.

e.g. India

e.g. skydiving

Guilt

- To learn about symbols in poetry;
- To understand what is meant by the word 'metaphysical';
- To reinforce understanding of style;
- To see how words can expand the imagination through word families and word banks;
- To learn what is meant by the words 'chant' and 'retort';
- To use a dictionary and a thesaurus.

Starter

As a class, talk about what guilt is and what it's like to feel guilty. What sorts of things do people do that they sometimes can't help but about which they still experience guilt? List as many examples as you can and be prepared to feed them back to the class.

FACT FILE

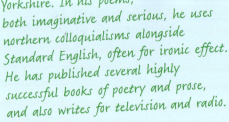

Simon Armitage is a prize-winning poet who was born in West Yorkshire. In his poems, both imaginative and serious, he uses northern colloquialisms alongside Standard English, often for ironic effect. He has published several highly successful books of poetry and prose, and also writes for television and radio.

Of 'Before You Cut Loose', the first poem in this unit, Armitage says: 'This is a poem about trying to get rid of something that just won't go away or be killed. The dog in this case is the hound of guilt.'

Before You Cut Loose

put dogs on the list
of difficult things to lose. Those dogs ditched
on the North York Moors or the Sussex Downs
or hurled like bags of sand from rented cars
have followed their noses to market towns
and bounced like balls into their owners' arms.
I heard one story of a dog that swam
to the English coast from the Isle of Man,
and a dog that carried eggs and bacon
and a morning paper from the village
surfaced umpteen leagues and two years later,
bacon eaten but the eggs unbroken,
newsprint dry as tinder, to the letter.
A dog might wander the width of the map
to bury its head in its owner's lap,
crawl the last mile to dab a bleeding paw
against its own front door. To die at home,
a dog might walk its four legs to the bone.
You can take off the tag and the collar
but a dog wears one coat and one colour.
A dog got rid of – that's a dog for life.
No dog howls like a dog kicked out at night.
Try looking a dog like that in the eye.

Simon Armitage

2 Introduction

Make notes on the following questions and be prepared to report back to the class.

■ Armitage is using the dog as a symbol of guilt that keeps on coming back in all sorts of ways. List the kind of qualities that are usually associated with dogs in terms of their relationships with humans. What kinds of things are the dogs in the poem doing?

■ How does the behaviour of the dogs add strength to what Armitage is trying to say about guilt?

■ If somebody 'cuts loose', what are they doing? To how many different examples of human behaviour can you apply this phrase? What might people 'cut loose' from?

■ Armitage constantly stresses the individual life of the dog: what it does, what it will do, how it will keep on coming back regardless. How is this similar to guilt?

■ In what form is the poem written? Why do you think the poet has used this form for this subject?

■ What do you think Armitage is saying in the lines 'You can take off the tag and the collar/but a dog wears one coat and one colour'?

3 Development

Powerful words create multiple images, leading to other ideas that expand our imagination. This is the essence of all good writing. The word 'bury', for instance, can mean submerge, sink, drown and so forms a layered imagery. Word banks and families can be found in a thesaurus where a dictionary may give us only a single-word definition.

Use a thesaurus to make flow charts to expand on the following words:

■ hurled

■ umpteen

■ crawl

■ howl

Now reread the poem and think about what is being said. Using quotations wherever possible, explain how Armitage:

■ gives the impression that the people are desperate to discard these 'dogs';

■ underlines the fact that the dogs are loyal;

■ makes it clear that they are almost impossible to escape.

Read the poem 'Nature and Free Animals', thinking about the way the words are spoken. Focus on how the poetry sounds. In what way is it different from other poems you have read? Stevie Smith rarely growls like Armitage does, but she often tries to laugh at things. In 'Nature and Free Animals', Smith has God talking to her, after which she makes a retort where she fiercely sticks up for herself.

Nature and Free Animals

I will forgive you everything,
But what you have done to my Dogs
I will not forgive.
You have taught them the sicknesses of your mind
And the sicknesses of your body
You have taught them to be servile
To hang servilely upon your countenance
To be dependent touching and entertaining
To have rights to be wronged
And wrongs to be righted.
You have taught them to be protected by a Society.
This I will not forgive,
Saith the Lord.
Well, God, it's all very well to talk like this
And I dare say it's all very fine
And Nature and Free Animals
Are all very fine,
Well all I can say is
If you wanted it like that
You shouldn't have created me
Not that I like it very much
And now that I'm on the subject I'll say,
What with Nature and Free Animals on the one side
And you on the other,
I hardly know I'm alive.

Stevie Smith

Introduction

Discuss the following questions in pairs and make notes on your answers.

- What have the dogs been taught by humans? List the things that are mentioned in the poem.
- Why might these things be unnatural?
- What does Stevie Smith have God saying to humans in the following lines:
  'You have taught them the sicknesses of your mind/And the sicknesses of your body/You have taught them to be servile'?
  Write notes in your own words to explain.
- How might dogs have been taught to have 'rights to be wronged/And wrongs to be righted'? Think of some examples of this and write them down. What do ideas like this tell you about guilty feelings?
- Why is God so angry that dogs have been made to need a 'Society' to protect them?

2 Development

A **retort** is an angry answer or retaliation to a charge made against someone. Looking at the retort the second speaker makes to what is said in the first half of the poem and the way she copes with the guilty sensations she experiences, write a short piece on how Smith feels when she is talking to God about dogs. Use the words below to help, looking them up in a dictionary if necessary.

surprised   bewildered   attacked   indignant
angry   guilty   misunderstood   responsible

3 Plenary

How is the dog's behaviour in 'Before You Cut Loose' a symbol of guilt?

In what ways do the two poems portray a dog as a kind of servant rather than a free creature?

Write down the different ways in which the two poets deal with guilt in the poems.

A **colloquial** word is a word that belongs to ordinary, familiar talk between certain groups of people and which might not be understood by others from a different place. Jot down two colloquial words that are used in 'Before You Cut Loose' and any others you can think of.

4 Homework

Compare and contrast the two poems, focusing on:

- what the dogs symbolise in each poem;
- how the poets treat the subject of guilt;
- the forms in which the poems have been written;
- which you enjoyed particularly and why.

Freedom

- To think about the difference between subject and theme in poetry;
- To look at how poets imagine and empathise;
- To reinforce understanding of rhyming couplets;
- To understand how the sestina form of poetry is written;
- To write a sestina.

1 Starter

On your own, spend three minutes writing as many adjectives as you can that you would associate with tigers. If it helps, think about the way they are depicted in films and on television.

Both the poems in this unit have a tiger as their subject, though the theme for each is different. One of the poems concentrates on the tiger's freedom and mystery; the other discusses the frustration and loss of liberty a tiger might feel in captivity.

FACT FILE

William Blake, a great mystical poet, was born in 1757 and died in 1827. He studied art at Pars' Drawing School in The Strand. He was first employed sketching monuments in Westminster Abbey from 1773 to 1778 before studying in the Antique School of the new Royal Academy. In 1780 he held his first exhibition of painting at the Royal Academy. In 1790 Blake began to use his Sketch Book to scribble down illustrations and later, in 1793, he began to note down poems, producing many of the great poems and paintings for which he is famous.

In 'The Tiger', William Blake describes with wonder the piercing freedom of the tiger in the night-time forest.

The Tiger

Tiger, tiger, burning bright,
In the forests of the night:
What immortal hand or eye
Could frame thy fearful symmetry?

In what distant deeps or skies,
Burnt the fire of thine eyes?
On what wings dare he aspire?
What the hand dare seize the fire?

And what shoulder, and what art,
Could twist the sinews of thy heart?
And when thy heart began to beat,
What dread hand? and what dread feet?

What the hammer? what the chain?
In what furnace was thy brain?
What the anvil? what dread grasp
Dare its deadly terrors clasp?

When the stars threw down their spears,
And watered Heaven with their tears,
Did he smile his work to see?
Did he who made the lamb make thee?

Tiger, tiger, burning bright,
In the forests of the night:
What immortal hand or eye
Dare frame thy fearful symmetry?

William Blake

Introduction

As a class, read the poem out loud, emphasising the exclamations and the questions to bring out the power of the words.

The poem is written in **rhyming couplets**. This means that each pair of lines has a rhyming word at the end, for example 'bright'/'night'. Writing in this form makes a poem move quickly. In what way do you think this suitable for the subject of Blake's poem?

Fire plays an important part in the poem. Draw the flame below into your books and write into it as many words as you can that describe a tiger's fearsomeness. Your words should contain sights, smells and sounds. Try to create as realistic a tiger as you can from your language. Two of the flames have been filled in for you.

predatory

sharp claws

Development

In groups, answer the following questions and make notes.

- What do you think Blake means when he asks 'What immortal hand or eye/Could frame thy fearful symmetry?'

- Where do you imagine the tiger's eyes have come from?

- Blake creates the image of the tiger's creator rising on wings, high enough to seize the fire he writes of out of the sky. What else does he say?

- Pick out all references to fire in the poem. Why do you think that these images have been used? What associations does 'fire' have?

- Think about the word 'symmetry'. Look it up in a dictionary and write a sentence to explain how Blake has used this word to describe the tiger. Why is the tiger's symmetry fearful?

- Blake writes about the tiger's brain being made in a furnace. What image do you have of its maker from these words?

- Why would the stars have thrown down their spears and cried when they saw the tiger. Why is saying the stars had spears such a clever idea?

Using the notes you have made, write a paragraph on the ways in which Blake presents the tiger as a fearsome creature.

FACT FILE

Hazel Streeter was born in 1987 in Torbay, South Devon. She moved to Scotland at the age of one and has continued to live there. Hazel says of her poem, 'The Captured Tiger': 'I wrote this poem in 1998 after reading an article on sestinas in a writing magazine, which said that this form of poetry can seem frustrated or restricted. I usually write in free verse but occasionally try [another] form as certain forms give me inspiration. I enjoy writing descriptive poems, especially about animals or people, and sometimes use rhyme to give my poems structure.'

The second poem, 'The Captured Tiger' by Hazel Streeter, is unlikely to use the words that we find in the poem by Blake, though both the poems show **empathy**. (To empathise is to try to imagine what it is like to be someone or something else.)

The poem is composed in the form of a sestina, and moves slowly and carefully, according to a set of rules. We can almost hear the tiger pacing the cage and losing its magic. Read the poem to yourself, then talk with a partner about how it is written.

The Captured Tiger

I see the tiger   (a)
and his waxing and waning shadow,   (b)
ever footsore, pacing   (c)
in the dirty, rusty cage,   (d)
his body bored;   (e)
his mind in the forest.   (f)

What a dream the forest   (f)
is for the lonely tiger,   (a)
a picture, but he's bored,   (e)
as a lengthening and shortening shadow   (b)
looms in and out of the cage,   (d)
as the tiger waits, pacing.   (c)

Pacing, ever pacing,   (c)
crying; 'Let me back to the forest!'   (f)
trapped, in a cage,   (d)
the helpless tiger,   (a)
looking into the shadow,   (b)
his mind always bored.   (e)

His limbs, bored   (e)
from endless pacing   (c)
around the only shadow;   (b)
beginning to give up hope of the forest,   (f)
the only home he knows, moth-eaten tiger,   (a)
in his steel-barred cage.   (d)

The broken cage   (d)
of no use, the tiger no longer bored,   (e)
an animal you can no longer call a tiger,   (a)
an animal, not up to pacing;   (c)
now his mind and soul are in the forest   (f)
the floor of the cage full of shadow.   (b)

I see in the shadow;   (b)
trapped in the cage;   (d)
mind in the forest;   (f)
a no longer bored,   (e)
no longer pacing,   (c)
sad and dying tiger.   (a)

The dead tiger   (a)
Lies in the lengthening shadows   (b)
Only its soul is free of pacing, ever pacing... (c)

Hazel Streeter

Introduction

 Make a star diagram in your book for 'The Captured Tiger', and place words on it that emphasise the tiger's weariness and imprisonment as seen in the poem.

footsore

captured tiger

Create a list of words from 'The Tiger' that contrast strongly with those on your diagram.

Using the ideas on your diagrams, add the words you have listed. Write a paragraph on:

- what is happening in the fifth stanza of 'The Captured Tiger';
- how this contrasts with the tiger in Blake's poem.

How to write a sestina

The form for a sestina looks complicated, though it is easy to use once you have mastered the rules. Let's see how they work.

The sestina is based on six words in six stanzas, each having six lines. Six lines are a sestet. Everything about the sestina revolves around six, so the form is called a sestina.

However, the final stanza has three lines only, rather than six like the others.

The important thing to remember about a sestina is that the final six words in the first stanza are repeated in a different order in each of the next five stanzas — it's a kind of game.

The six end words Hazel has chosen for 'The Captured Tiger' are: 'tiger', 'shadow', 'pacing', 'cage', 'bored' and 'forest'. Look at the poem and see how these words are placed at the end of each line in the first stanza. The same words are at the end of each line in the other stanzas but in a different order:

Stanza 1: a, b, c, d, e, f

Stanza 2: f, a, e, b, d, c

Stanza 3: c, f, d, a, b, e

Stanza 4: e, c, b, f, a, d

Stanza 5: d, e, a, c, f, b

Stanza 6: b, d, f, e, c, a

The final stanza of three lines should match with two each of the letters in the sixth stanza; one in the middle and one at the end, as: b, d/f, e/c, a. But Hazel has strayed from the rules! Work out the code and see. When you are writing your own sestina later, try to stay with the pattern.

2 Development

With a partner, look at how 'The Captured Tiger' is formed, then try to write a sestina together. You could use the following six words:

- girl
- swinging
- trapeze
- circus
- lights
- people

You might line the words up in six lines, then put them where you think they should go in the stanzas that follow. Then you can create the rest of the words yourself and the last three-line stanza. Here is an example of how a first stanza might go:

I can see the girl.

She is swinging

on the high trapeze,

dizzy in the circus.

It is full of bright lights

and excited people.

When you have written your poem, exchange it with another pair in your class and ask for comments. Make any changes that seem necessary and, after redrafting, take turns to read the poem aloud to your friend and see how it flows.

3 Plenary

What do you understand by the term 'sestina'? What is the number it revolves around?

Explain what is meant by a 'rhyming couplet'.

Give three examples of 'forms' a poem might take.

What does it mean to say that the narrator in 'The Captured Tiger' is empathising with the tiger in the poem? Is Blake empathising with the tiger too?

Whilst the subject of both poems is a tiger, what are the different themes covered by the poets? (The theme is what is being considered with regard to the subject.)

4 Homework

Using a form that you feel comfortable with, choose an animal to write about and create a poem to explore your thoughts on the creature. It may help to make a star diagram or a flowchart to organise your ideas.

Learning

AIMS

- To understand the meaning of irony;

- To reinforce the idea of what a monologue means;

- To become aware of philosophy as applied to poetry;

- To understand the meaning of perspective;

- To look at the different ways of learning;

- To think about the limitations of learning from books;

- To consider the different positions and circumstances of those involved in the learning process;

- To compare words from different times in history;

- To understand how poetry is different from prose;

- To reinforce understanding of colloquial language and standard English;

- To learn to write a review and prepare a brief talk in preparation for GCSE.

This unit concentrates on the different things that happen in the learning process and how they are all important.

 Starter

 In small groups, write down four things that are very important in the learning process. (One might be a good teacher! But what else?) Choose someone from your group to read out what you have chosen to the rest of the class, then make notes of any ideas given by others you hadn't thought of yourself.

The first poem in this unit, by William Wordsworth, is light-hearted and philosophical – as were many of the poems of his day. Read the poem to yourself then answer the questions that follow.

FACT FILE

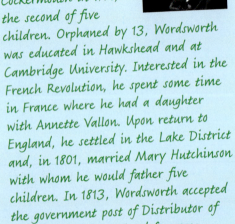

William Wordsworth was born in Cockermouth in 1771, the second of five children. Orphaned by 13, Wordsworth was educated in Hawkshead and at Cambridge University. Interested in the French Revolution, he spent some time in France where he had a daughter with Annette Vallon. Upon return to England, he settled in the Lake District and, in 1801, married Mary Hutchinson with whom he would father five children. In 1813, Wordsworth accepted the government post of Distributor of Stamps for Westmorland for some much-needed money. He continued writing poetry, however, and became Poet Laureate in 1843 until his death in 1850.

The Tables Turned

Up! up! my Friend, and quit your books;
Or surely you'll grow double:
Up! up! my Friend, and clear your looks;
Why all this toil and trouble?

The sun, above the mountain's head,
A freshening lustre mellow
Through all the long green fields has spread,
His first sweet evening yellow.

Books! 'tis a dull and endless strife;
Come, hear the woodland linnet,
How sweet his music! on my life,
There's more of wisdom in it.

And hark! how blithe the throstle sings!
He, too, is no mean preacher:
Come forth into the light of things,
Let Nature be your Teacher.

She has a world of ready wealth,
Our minds and hearts to bless –
Spontaneous wisdom breathed by health,
Truth breathed by cheerfulness.

One impulse from a vernal wood
May teach you more of man,
Of moral evil and of good,
Than all the sages can.

Sweet is the lore which Nature brings;
Our meddling intellect
Mis-shapes the beauteous forms of things: –
We murder to dissect.

Enough of Science and of Art;
Close up those barren leaves;
Come forth, and bring with you a heart
That watches and receives.

William Wordsworth

 Introduction

 Read the poem aloud as a class. Then, in your
 groups, make notes on the following questions.

■ What will you gain if you leave your books and venture out into nature? List all the things that Wordsworth suggests.

■ What does he say will happen to you if you stay with your books? Again, list his ideas.

■ The title of the poem is 'The Tables Turned'. Why do you think that the poet has chosen this title?

■ What might the modern versions be for the following words: hark, blithe, come forth, sage, lore?

■ The first line of each stanza in 'The Tables Turned' rhymes with the third line, the second line rhymes with the fourth line, and so on. This gives a marching pace to the poem. Why is this rhyme scheme so suitable for Wordsworth's poem?

■ In the fourth stanza, Wordsworth writes about 'the light of things'. What do you think he means by these words? What are his reasons for suggesting that nature is a better teacher than a book?

■ Wordsworth says that 'our meddling intellect' kills things by trying to find out about them. Why do you think this might happen? Discuss his words and make notes on your answer.

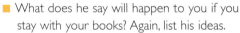 Development

 Write down a definition of what you think Wordsworth means by 'spontaneous wisdom'. How might this be different from wisdom learned from books?

Wordsworth is being philosophical in this poem. He is playfully questioning values held by many people. In your own words, try to write down the argument he is putting forward, using quotations from the poem to support what you say.

 Organise a debate on 'the lore which nature brings' versus 'knowledge learned from books'.

The second poem is also about learning, but it discusses it from a different angle. The speaker in Fleur Adock's poem is learning about herself. She learns this from her situation, and from her thinking.

Of her poem, 'Chippenham', Fleur Adcock says: 'The poem reflects a time in 1944 when I was unofficially evacuated to Wiltshire for a few months to escape the Doodlebugs (flying bombs) which were attacking south-east England. The woman I was billeted with had a toddler who couldn't pronounce my name, and she therefore called me Jean. Her cottage was small and rather primitive, with no running water. Hygiene and education both came rather low in her priorities; she kept me home from school, more often than not, for company.'

FACT FILE

Fleur Adcock was born in Auckland in 1934. She spent the war years in England but returned to Wellington in 1947. She has published many successful collections of poetry and was awarded an OBE in 1996. Her work ranges from carefully-rhymed verse to easy conversational pieces, her themes covering nature, love, domestic life and other subjects with both gentle shrewdness and sharp attack.

Chippenham

The maths master was eight feet tall.
He jabbed his clothes'-prop arm at me
halfway across the classroom, stretched
his knobbly finger, shouted 'You!

You're only here one day in three,
and when you are you might as well
not be, for all the work you do!
What do you think you're playing at?'

What did I think? I shrank into
my grubby blouse. Who did I think
I was, among these blazered boys,
these tidy girls in olive serge?

My green skirt wasn't uniform:
clothes were on coupons, after all.
I'd get a gymslip – blue, not green –
for Redhill Grammar, some time soon

when we went home. But, just for now,
what did I think? I thought I was
betrayed. I thought of how I'd stood
an hour waiting for the bus

that morning, by a flooded field,
watching the grass-blades drift and sway
beneath the water like wet hair;
hoping for Mrs Johnson's call:

'Jean, are you there? The clock was wrong.
You've missed the bus.' And back I'd run
to change my clothes, be Jean again,
play with the baby, carry pails

of water from the village tap,
go to the shop, eat toast and jam,
and then, if she could shake enough
pennies and farthings from her bag,

we might get to the pictures. But
the clock was fast, it seemed, not slow;
the bus arrived; and as I slid
anonymously into it

an elegant male prefect said
'Let Fleur sit down, she's got bad feet.'
I felt my impetigo scabs
blaze through my shoes. How did he know?

Fleur Adcock

1 Introduction

Make notes on the following questions and be prepared to discuss your answers with the class.

- The poet describes the maths master as being 'eight feet tall' and having an arm like a 'clothes-prop'. What do these descriptions tell you about her feelings?

- The teacher asks the Fleur what she thinks she is 'playing at'. What impression is given of the way the girl is feeling when she says 'What did I think?'

- The words 'playing at' are **colloquial** words. This means they are the words you would expect to hear in everyday conversation. In standard English, what is the teacher really saying? Is Fleur really 'playing' at all?

- How does the narrator compare herself to her classmates? Look at the adjectives she uses to describe them and her. How might this underline her feeling of isolation?

- What does Fleur think about her situation? Is she angry, embarrassed, ashamed, or is she just indifferent? Quote lines from the poem to support what you write and look up any difficult words in a dictionary.

- What does 'Jean' have to do a lot of the time that isn't concerned with school? Do you think she feels she 'belongs' at the school, or is something else suggested? Why do you think the name 'Jean' is mentioned, and then the name 'Fleur'?

- Which word from the penultimate (the next to last) stanza helps to create, by contrast, surprise at the end of the poem?

2 Development

The tension in Adcock's poem is built cleverly into the writing by the way she hangs onto the words, creating full rhymes and half rhymes, and winding them in together. It is almost as if she is trying to run, then catch her breath. Read the poem again.

In line 4 of the first stanza, 'finger' makes a loose rhyme, with 'are' in line 2 of the second stanza. 'Bus' at the end of the fifth stanza is a loose rhyme with 'grass' in the second line of the sixth stanza, and 'hair' is a full rhyme with 'there' in the seventh stanza. The eighth stanza has 'jam' loosely rhyming with 'and then' in the third line. All these rhyming techniques help to create the emotion in the poem.

Reading 'Chippenham' we can 'feel' and therefore empathise with the narrator. Using the diagram below, copy the lines from the poem into your book and write down how the narrator is feeling. Then write down how you feel yourself as you read them.

Lines from the poem	The narrator's feelings	My own feelings
'You're only here one day in three, and when you are you might as well not be, for all the work you do!'	The girl is feeling nervous and confused. She might also be angry.	I feel sympathy for her because the master is shouting at her. I want to know what's going to happen.
'...Who did I think I was, among these blazered boys, These tidy girls in olive serge?'		
'that morning, by a flooded field, watching the grass-blades drift and sway beneath the water like wet hair;'		
'... And back I'd run to change my clothes, be Jean again, play with the baby, carry pails'		
'an elegant male prefect said 'Let Fleur sit down, she's got bad feet.' I felt my impetigo scabs blaze through my shoes. How did he know?'		

The third poem, 'Dead Thick' by Brian Patten, takes on the persona of an English teacher and delivers an ironic monologue.

Dead Thick

No. I haven't kept up with the modern stuff.
Haven't read a book in years.
Textbooks? A few, but nothing new.
Mind you, it's not that I don't
have the inclination, just that
Nothing's grabbed my fancy.

Still, I like what I've read: Hardy,
Golding, I'll flick through
Graham Greene if I have to.
But no, nothing new. Mind you
I read the reviews. They contain
A lot of sharp observation.
After reading a couple I find
I can form my own opinion.

I'm too busy for literature, that's the problem.
I'm after promotion. Ideally what I'd like
Is a job in administration.
What do I do? Teach. English.
It's exhausting. The kids are thick.
They've nothing between their ears.
Do you know what? Some of them
Haven't read a book in years.

Brian Patten

FACT FILE

Brian Patten was born in 1946 in Liverpool where he was brought up. An award-winning poet, he has published many adult poetry collections and also writes poems for children. He writes on themes of love, nature, spirituality, otherworldliness, and – often to ironic effect – school. Patten is one of the Liverpool Poets, together with Roger McGough and Adrian Henri. Patten's work has been translated into many languages.

Irony is when words are said that really mean something else, and a **monologue** is a speech delivered by one person. The word 'monologue' comes from the Greek word 'monologus' which means 'speaking alone'. If we break the word into two, the first part, the prefix, is from the word 'mono' meaning 'alone', and the suffix 'logue' is from the Greek word 'logos' meaning 'word'. This way you can see how the word has evolved. Both Brian Patten and William Wordsworth have written about books in their poems but each from a different perspective. Both of the poems are monologues.

Of his poem, 'Dead Thick', Brian Patten says: ' 'Dead Thick' is about a real 'teacher' (that's the wrong word for him though) who I met in a staff-room when I was visiting a school to do a reading ages ago.'

Introduction

Read the poem as a class. Then, in your groups, discuss the questions below and make notes on your answers.

■ Does the teacher enjoy the job? Scan the poem for lines to support your answer.

■ Patten refers to certain authors in the poem. Does the narrator read them for pleasure? Give reasons for your answer.

■ What impression do you get from the fact that the teacher will 'flick through' these authors?

■ The teacher says that 'Nothing's grabbed my fancy'. Do you think this is true?

- Why do you think the teacher is 'too busy for literature,' or doesn't have time for 'the modern stuff'?

- Why do you think the teacher reads the reviews? What do the words 'After reading a couple I find/I can form my own opinion' suggest?

- A good example of irony is when the teacher says 'The kids are thick' and that some of them 'Haven't read a book in years'. Why you think this is?

- Patten uses everyday language in his poem. Many of the words and phrases used are colloquial. Can you find two colloquial words and two colloquial lines? Write them down together with their standard English equivalent. (Standard English is a way of speaking that everyone understands and often used for formal speech and important documents.)

- What is the effect of writing the poem in conversational (colloquial) language? Where might the teacher be saying these words? Do you think he would want to be quoted?

 **Development**

 From the words in the following list, pick out the three that best describe the teacher:

tired   disillusioned   disinterested
self-interested   out-of-touch   uninspired
ignorant   unimaginative   tongue-in-cheek
cynical

Write a paragraph on each word you have chosen, explaining why it is a suitable word for this teacher. Use evidence from the poem to support your argument.

 **Plenary**

Write down the title of each poem and, choosing words from the list below, match them to whichever poem you think they best fit. Some may apply to more than one.

satirical   amusing   tearful   nostalgic
thoughtful   homesick   sulky   embarrassed
cross   strong   amusing   sensitive   solemn
self-willed   careless   defensive   playful
light-hearted   serious   philosophical   happy

Now write notes to answer the following questions.

- In which of the poems is a sense of the need to escape most pronounced?

- Can you find two words from the Wordsworth poem and two words from one of the other poems to show how language has changed over time?

- Can you suggest three different ways of learning that are equally valid?

- What might you learn from watching TV or talking to someone that you could not learn from a book? Think of one time you learned something, just from experience.

 **Homework**

 Prepare a draft review of one of the three poems focusing on:

- what the poem is about;
- the language and why the poet has used it;
- whether you think it's effective;
- the form of the poem and the rhyme scheme;
- what you like about the poem, explaining why.

Take turns to read your review to the rest of the class and prepare yourself to answer questions. Listen to others and try to ask relevant questions on what they have written.

or

Write a poem about a time when you were made to feel embarrassed in front of people. Think about what happened and how you felt.

AIMS

- To reinforce the meaning of a monologue;

- To understand the term 'standard English';

- To compare standard English, argot and dialect and see how they are different;

- To reinforce understanding of theme and form in poetry;

- To give a brief talk in preparation for GCSE orals.

The three poems in this unit are all about mothers. Jackie Kay in 'The Telling Part' and Benjamin Zephaniah in 'I Love Me Mudder' are both recounting something that is important to them that concerns their mother. Christopher Reid in 'Memres of Alfred Stoker' is relating an old man's memories about something his mother told him. His poem uses argot, which is a kind of jargon used by a small group, such as a family.

The poems are not written in standard English – that is, so called 'correct' English – but instead are in a free-flowing, easy language developed from the informal way that people speak to each other.

1 Starter

 As a class, discuss the language used by small children. Is there any argot used in your family, which only the family members understand? Make a list of the secret words and why you continue to use them.

As a class, how many different accents and dialects can you name?

FACT FILE

Benjamin Zephaniah was born and raised in Birmingham. His poetry is strongly influenced by the music and poetry of Jamaica and what he calls 'street politics'. He is very much a performance poet and has published many poetry books, as well as books in prose, musical recordings and plays for both radio and television. He is also an actor and patron for societies like The Prison Phoenix Trust, which promotes yoga and meditation in prisons.

I Love Me Mudder

I love me mudder and me mudder love me
we come so far from over de sea
we heard dat de streets were paved with gold
sometime it hot sometime it cold,

I love me mudder and me mudder love me
we try fe live in harmony
you might know her as Valerie
but to me she is my mummy.

She shouts at me daddy so loud some time
she stays fit and she don't drink wine
she always do the best she can
she work damn hard down ina England,

she's always singing some kind of song
she have big muscles and she very very strong,
she likes pussy cats and she love cashew nuts
she don't bother with no ifs and buts.

I love me mudder and me mudder love me
we come so far from over de sea
we heard dat de streets were paved with gold
sometime it hot sometime it cold,

I love her and she love me too
and dis is a love I know is true
my family unit extends to you
loving each other is the ting to do

Benjamin Zephaniah

Jackie Kay's poem is a mixture of Scottish **dialect** *and* **standard English**. *Dialect is a language that springs from where people live and is sometimes hard for those who do not live there to understand. Benjamin Zephaniah's poem is also in dialect. Dialects often have words arranged in unusual ways, and can be spoken in an accent. You may have heard of Lancashire and Cockney dialects but there are many others. The most important thing about dialects is the way the words are spoken, and you will rarely find these dialectal words in a dictionary.*

By contrast, Christopher Reid's poem has been written in **argot** *and is spoken in the persona of an old man. Argot is a language that can be like a code that will be understood by certain people. It may contain* **slang** *or* **jargon**. *Particular groups of people sometimes develop their own argot to hide what they say. More commonly though, argot is ordinary language which has been garbled. Families may do this with a word by changing its sound, or cutting out syllables, so that only they can understand what is being said. Small children often use their own words for things. The family often continues the word and it becomes part of their vocabulary though no one outside the family understands it.*

 **Introduction**

 Read the poem as a class. In your groups, list as many things as you can that Benjamin Zephaniah says about his mother.

 Judging from the information you can extract from the poem, write a description of the kind of person the poet's mother is.

What is the poet saying in the lines 'we heard dat de streets were paved with gold/sometime it hot sometime it cold'?

 **Development**

 In your groups, make notes in answer to the following questions.

■ The poem is written in dialect. In what ways does writing the poem like this enable the poet to say things that would otherwise lose something in standard English? Imagine how this poem would read in standard English. What could you say about it?

■ Why do you think that writers write in dialect? In what ways might it be an important statement of who they are? Can you name any other writers who write in English but not standard English, other than the other two poets in this unit?

■ Benjamin Zephaniah is well known as a performance poet. Read the poem again and concentrate on the rhyming. Why is this poem especially suitable for performing? Give reasons for your answer.

FACT FILE

Jackie Kay was born in Edinburgh and grew up in Glasgow. She has published three collections of poetry and won the Saltire and Forward prizes for 'The Adoption Papers'. She has also won a Somerset Maugham Award and been shortlisted for the T. S. Eliot prize. In addition, she writes novels and short stories. Jackie Kay now lives in Manchester.

Of her poem, 'The Telling Part', the poet says: 'This poem is part of a longer narrative poem, 'The Adoption Papers'. I liked trying to explore the three voices of birth mother, adoptive mother and daughter.'

The Telling Part

Ma mammy bot me oot a shop
Ma mammy says I was a luvly baby

Ma mammy picked me (I wiz the best)
your mammy had to take you (she'd no choice)

Ma mammy says she's no really ma mammy
(just kid on)

It's a bit like a part you've rehearsed so well
you can't play it on the opening night
She says my real mammy is away far away
Mammy why aren't you and me the same colour
    But I love my mammy whether she's real or no
My heart started rat tat tat like a tin drum
all the words took off to another planet
Why

But I love ma mammy whether she's real or no

I could hear the upset in her voice
I says *I'm not your real mother*
though Christ knows why I said that
If I'm not who is, but all my planned speech
went out the window

She took me when I'd nowhere to go
  my mammy is the best mammy in the world OK

After mammy telt me she wisnae my real mammy
I was scared to death she was gonnie melt
or something or mibbe disappear in the dead
of night and somebody would say she wis a fairy
godmother. So the next morning I felt her skin
to check it was flesh, but mibbe it was just
a good imitation. How could I tell my mammy
was a dummy with a voice spoken by someone else
So I searches the whole house for clues
but I never found nothing. Anyhow a day after
I got my guinea pig and forgot all about it.

I always believed in the telling anyhow.
You can't keep something like that secret
I wanted her to think of her other mother
out there thinking that child I had will be
seven today eight today all the way up to
god knows when. I told my daughter –
I bet your mother's never missed your birthday
How could she?

Jackie Kay

Introduction

 In groups, discuss the following questions and make notes on your answers.

- In 'The Telling Part', there is more than one person talking. Who are the people and who they are talking to?

- In the first part of the poem, things that 'mammy' has done are listed. Do you believe any of them? If so, why?

- Whose heart beats like a 'tin drum'? Why does it beat this way? What is happening?

- Why might the narrators in 'The Telling Part' feel less secure than the one in 'I Love Me Mudder'?

- **Why do you think these two poems are in dialect? Thinking about the themes will help you with your answer.**

- **What kind of form are the poems written in?**

- **Why has 'The Telling Part' been written in a mixture of dialect and standard English? What is the effect of this?**

- Make a list of the dialect words in 'The Telling Part', then give the standard English equivalent for each.

Development

 'I Love Me Mudder' is a monologue in that it is a speech presented by one person only. Try to find ways in which the poem is different from 'The Telling Part'. Look at the words below and match them to each of the poems. This will help you to see the mood of the poem. (Some of the words may apply to both.)

happy   sad   dancing   melancholy   serious   brave   strong   loving   funny

Using the notes you have made, compare and contrast 'I Love Me Mudder' with 'The Telling Part'. Make sure that you cover the following points:

- what the poems are about;
- the language used;
- the forms the poems are written in;
- which you particularly enjoyed and why.

> **Standard English** is a way of speaking that everyone understands. Although it is the form of language used by most people, some of the words can be long and formal, and are sometimes only found in business documents or for talking about serious issues. This is why dialects develop. People want to communicate quickly in their own way and therefore create a 'short cut' to communication.

FACT FILE

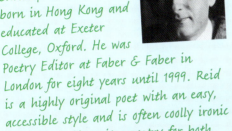

Christopher Reid was born in Hong Kong and educated at Exeter College, Oxford. He was Poetry Editor at Faber & Faber in London for eight years until 1999. Reid is a highly original poet with an easy, accessible style and is often coolly ironic and warm. He writes poetry for both adults and children.

The third poem in this unit is an extract from 'Memres of Alfred Stoker', a long poem in which Alfred, one hundred years old and talking in **argot**, relates something his mother has told him. He begins his narrative by telling us when he was born and what happened. This poem is also a monologue since it is a story told to us by Alfred. The word 'monologue' comes from the Greek word 'monologus' which means 'speaking alone'.

Memres of Alfred Stoker

firs
born X mas day
Yer 1885
in the same burer Waping

pa a way
Ma not
being by Trade merchent Sea man
in forn parts:
all so a precher
on Land

i sow him Latter

4 of 9
not all Livig

a hard Thing Ma sad:
mirs Pale a mid Wife
in the back room bed rom
Nor wod she got Thurgh
when a ANGEL apperd over the JESUS pichire
which i got after
it Savd my Life.

so i name Gabriel
which you did not no why shod you
onlie its Secd
Alfred Gabriel Joseph Stoker
Like that.

some recked she was Ling
but she was not
the ANGEL was Trew.

He had a Gold face she sad
and his Winges Gold flammy
and his ramond of Gold stufes

and in his hand he bare a BIBLE of Gold paper
and his Vois was as the Claper of Tunder over hede
with Gold Litnigg to.

pa rejoyd when he come
and spid the mars Like Candles smut
on the bed room Cornes

Than Ma had Gerge Edie Peg so on
but no ANGEL.

Christopher Reid

Introduction

In small groups, choose someone to read the poem aloud. Listen carefully to the sounds of the words and try to understand them. Then write what you think the words below mean:

burer   forn   sow   sad   wod   Thurgh
recked   Ling   ramond

■ Discuss what Alfred means when he says his father rejoiced when he 'spid the mars Like Candles smut' in the bedroom corners.

■ Why wasn't it the same when Alfred's siblings were born? What does he say?

■ What can you say about sound and spelling in 'Memres of Alfred Stoker'?

■ What do you really think about Alfred's story?

Development

Copy the chart below into your books. Find words from 'Memres of Alfred Stoker' to describe what the standard English is saying. The first has been done for you.

Standard English prose	'Memres of Alfred Stoker'
My father was overseas.	*pa a way* *being a Trade merchent Sea man* *in forn parts*
My mother would never have got through my birth.	
Gabriel is my second name.	
The angel was in gold raiment.	
My father was overjoyed when he saw the marks, like the stains from candles, in the corners of the bedroom walls.	

Write the following headings in your books: 'I Love me Mudder', 'The Telling Part' and 'Memries of Alfred Stoker'. From the phrases below, pick out those which best describe the main themes of the three poems and list them under the correct heading/s. (Some of the phrases may apply to more than one poem.)

- Closeness between parent and child;
- Unconditional love;
- Nervousness about being alone;
- Vivid imagination;
- Strength in the mother figure;
- Worry about identity;
- The special place of a mother;
- Fear that the mother may disappear;
- Long distance travel;
- Adopting an animal for security.

 **Plenary**

What is meant by the term 'standard English'?

How is standard English different from argot and dialect?

What is a monologue?

What is meant by the terms 'theme' and 'form'?

Try to think of some argot that is used in your family and write it down.

 **Homework**

Reread the three poems, then write a short story about something somebody told you that had previously been a secret. You should include the following points from the writing frame below.

Writing frame

- How I felt when they told me.
- Other people involved.
- The place where I was told.
- The atmosphere at the time they told me.
- The way they were feeling.
- What they said.
- The tone of their voice.
- Why they told me.
- What I said to them.
- What we decided to do.

See if you can introduce argot, dialect or colloquial language into your story, as well as standard English.

War

■ To see how choice of language can create a particular atmosphere;

■ To develop skills in using text based evidence to support your personal views and observations about poems;

■ To learn how to write a commentary making comparisons between poems;

■ To improve skills of rehearsing and delivering a talk in preparation for GCSE orals.

1 Starter

Poetry about war and conflict is often written as a way of responding to the tense emotions experienced at such times. Each of the following poems has something different to say, and creates its own individual comment and atmosphere.

As a class, discuss why poets might want to write about war. Think of fears you would have in a time of war that you would not need to think about in times of peace. List five of these possible fears.

This poem by Wilfred Owen captures in haunting imagery the horrors of trench warfare during the First World War.

FACT FILE

Wilfred Owen was born in 1893 in Oswestry. He went to school in Birkenhead and Shrewsbury. After the outbreak of the First World War, he decided to enlist. Commissioned into the Manchester Regiment, Owen went to France and joined the 2nd Manchesters on the Somme near Beaumont Hamel. He was awarded the Military Cross for his part in the fighting and led his platoon to the west bank of the Sambre and Oise Canal in November 1917. At the height of the battle, Owen was hit by a machine gun bullet and killed.

Dulce Et Decorum Est

Bent double, like old beggars under sacks,
Knock-kneed, coughing like hags, we cursed through sludge,
Till on the haunting flares we turned our backs
And towards our distant rest began to trudge.
Men marched asleep. Many had lost their boots
But limped on, blood-shod. All went lame; all blind;
Drunk with fatigue; deaf even to the hoots
Of tired, outstripped Five-Nines that dropped behind.

Gas! GAS! Quick, boys! – An ecstasy of fumbling,
Fitting the clumsy helmets just in time;
But someone still was yelling out and stumbling
And flound'ring like a man in fire or lime…
Dim, through the misty panes and thick green light,
As under a green sea, I saw him drowning.

In all my dreams, before my helpless sight,
He plunges at me, guttering, choking, drowning.

If in some smothering dreams you too could pace
Behind the wagon that we flung him in,
And watch the white eyes writhing in his face,
His hanging face, like a devil's sick of sin;
If you could hear, at every jolt, the blood
Come gargling from the froth-corrupted lungs,
Obscene as cancer, bitter as the cud
Of vile, incurable sores on innocent tongues, –
My friend, you would not tell with such high zest
To children ardent for some desperate glory,
The old Lie: Dulce et decorum est
Pro patria mori.

Wilfred Owen

In his poem, Owen describes the effects of a gas attack and the consequences for one unfortunate young soldier. Owen used his poetry to challenge the patriotic view that many people had of war back in Britain. The heroic nature of battle and the importance of fighting for the country were popular images when Owen was writing. 'Dulce Et Decorum Est', the title of the poem, is taken from the words 'Dulce et decorum est pro patria mori', meaning 'It is lovely and honourable to die for your country'. These famous lines were written in Latin by the Roman poet, Horace, and became a popular motto for generations of young British men faced with having to fight for their country.

Introduction

Answer the following questions in your groups and make notes on your answer.

- Does Owen really believe that 'Dulce et decorum est pro patria mori' is true? Copy some lines from the poem to support your answer.

- Why do you think he has chosen this motto for the poem's title?

- Find the words that help create a horrific picture of the realities of battle. How do they add to the ugliness of the scene? Pick out as many phrases as you can that tell us of the appalling situation of the men.

- In his poem, Owen attempts to recreate the brutal horrors of war. To build powerful and realistic images into his writing he chooses words and phrases that conjure up the reality of how it was. Scan the poem for the words 'sludge', 'trudge' and 'blood-shod'. Note down the images that come to your mind when you read them. In what ways do the sounds of these words add to their meaning?

- In the last stanza, Owen writes 'My friend'. Who do you think he means when he says this? Why does he use the word 'ardent' when he writes

about the feelings of the children who are being told stories of war? In what ways might this word be dangerous later on, and how does it apply to the title of Owen's poem? Use a dictionary for any words you find difficult.

- Find two similes in the poem that add to the sense of being smothered by war.

Development

Using the notes you have made, write a paragraph on each of the following. Use quotations from the poem wherever possible.

- The conditions in the trenches and the condition of the men;
- The way the death of the soldier is described;
- The language that Owen has used to depict the warfare in the trenches;
- What you think Owen's attitude to war is and how he makes his views clear.

In your groups, organise a debate around the title of this poem. You should find out as much as you can about pro- and anti-war campaigns, including any relevant contemporary events.

Write a 'group poem' to show how you feel about the point of view your side is putting forward. Be prepared to read your poem to the class before you debate.

FACT FILE

The poet Gladys Mary Coles has won many awards and competitions for her richly-varied work. Her themes include people, places and personal experience. She has published several highly-successful poetry collections and is a regular adjudicator for poetry competitions, as well as Director of Headland Publications.

Of this poem, Gladys Mary Coles says: 'The inspiration for 'The Dornier' was a photograph I found in a newspaper a few years ago. It is of a Welsh farmer finding two unexploded bombs from the Second World War when ploughing his field. I researched the subject and discovered that a German bomber plane – a Dornier – had crashed in that part of North Wales. These facts were the basis of the poem in which I have attempted to say something about the disruption of rural peace in wartime. The poem is a monologue in the voice of the farmer.'

The Dornier

The moorland blazing and a bomber's moon
lit skies light as a June dawn,
the harvest stubble to a guilty flush.
I saw from the farmhouse the smoking plane
like a giant bat in a sideways dive,
fuel spewing from its underbelly.
I remember how one wing tipped our trees
tearing the screen of pines like lace,
flipping over, flimsy as my balsa models.
It shattered on the pasture, killing sheep,
ripping the fence where the shot fox hung.
Dad let me look next morning at the wreck –
it lay in two halves like a broken wasp,
nose nestled in the ground, blades
of the propellers bent…
I thought I saw them moving
in the wind.

If the Invader comes, the leaflet said,
*Do not give a German anything. Do not tell him
anything. Hide your food and bicycles.
Hide your maps. …* But these Luftwaffe men
were dead. Their machine, a carcass
cordoned off. A museum dinosaur.
Don't go nearer. Do not touch.

Trophies, I took – a section of the tail
(our collie found it dangling in the hedge),
pieces of perspex like thin ice on the grass,
some swapped for shrapnel down at school
(how strangely it burned in a slow green flame).
Inscribed *September 1940, Nantglyn,*
the black-crossed relic now hangs on our wall.
My son lifts it down, asks questions
I can't answer.

Yesterday, turning the far meadow for new drains,
our blades hit three marrows, huge and hard,
stuffed with High Explosive – the Dornier's final gift.
Cordoned off, they're photographed, defused.
I take my son to see the empty crater,
the imprint of their shapes still in the soil –
shadows that turn up time.

Gladys Mary Coles

(Note: A Dornier is a German bomber plane.)

1 Introduction

Gladys Mary Coles did not actually witness this incident. She is therefore **empathising** with the situation. Empathy is when someone seems to participate in an event in their imagination because they can feel it keenly, even if they haven't experienced it directly themselves. Because she is telling the story, the poet here is the narrator, though she narrates the tale in the voice of the farmer with whom she is empathising.

With your partner, make notes to answer the following questions.

- How do you know who is speaking in this poem? Find words, lines and phrases to support what you say.
- Another voice appears in this poem, emphasised by italic print. Whose voice is it?
- Why might the harvest stubble be described as 'a guilty flush'?
- Why might a piece of the plane be a trophy to a child?
- The plane crash brings signs of war to the farm. Which images used from the first stanza underline the destruction that the Dornier has brought with it? Look carefully at the language used and list the images.

2 Development

Compare the voices in this poem with the voice that is used in 'Dulce Et Decorum Est'. What can you say about the tone and urgency of the two poems?

The two poems both describe dramatic events: a gas attack and a plane crash. Look closely at the different styles of writing and think about the following lines:

- 'Gas! GAS! Quick, boys! –'
  What effect is Owen trying to create by choosing this way of writing? What do you notice about the words?
- 'flipping over, flimsy as my balsa models' and 'it lay in two halves like a broken wasp'.
  How does the style of language used by Gladys Mary Coles differ from that of Owen? Saying the lines aloud might help. How quickly do you read them? Do you want to deliver them softly or with a shout?

The following words describe how the poem is written. Match them to either 'The Dornier' or 'Dulce Et Decorum Est'. Discuss your choices.

- The dramatic event is described in a close up, personal way;
- The dramatic event is a horrific memory;
- The poet writes about the event in a calm manner;
- The poet's writing is **subjective**;
- The poem contains some beautiful images;
- The imagery in the poem is ugly.;
- The poet is thinking **objectively**.

In 'Starter's Orders', Mick Imlah's view of war is very different from that explored in the other two poems. Time has moved on and he reflects on how young men today might 'waste themselves'.

Starter's Orders

These warless days
Men without women
Thirst for the means
To waste themselves;

It's in the blood.
Their fathers worked
And Grandad breasted
A barbed tape;

But now where the girls
Are sick of courage
Men without hope
Of a job, or a bayonet,

Muster like champions
Under a canopy,
Over a barrel,
Primed for the slaughter;

Fit to pursue
Illness, dishonour,
And sponsored to boot.
Gentlemen, swallow!

Mick Imlah

FACT FILE

Mick Imlah was born in Scotland in 1956 and was brought up in Milngavie and London. He read English at Magdalen College, Oxford. He has been editor of 'Oxford Poetry', 'Poetry Review' and Poetry Editor for Chatto & Windus, and is at present Poetry Editor for the 'Times Literary Supplement'. Imlah is said to take pleasure in the play element of language, as well as enjoying the employment of formal skill. He has published two poetry collections and is also an anthologist.

1 Introduction

 With a partner, make notes to answer the following questions.

- Which generations do you think the poet is referring to? Give reasons for your answer.

- Imlah maintains that 'Their fathers worked'. Why might the men he refers to be without hope of a job?

- The word 'thirst' is used in the first stanza. How effective is this word when thinking about the poem?

- What do you understand by 'It's in the blood'?

- What kind of 'courage' might the girls be sick of? What type of behaviour does this imply?

- How does the title 'Starter's Orders' add to the meaning of the poem?

2 Development

 In your pairs, discuss the following lines and note down what you understand by them:

- 'And Grandad breasted/A barbed tape'
- 'Muster like champions'
- 'And sponsored to boot./Gentlemen, swallow!'

Mick Imlah is putting forward an argument in his poem. Write this argument down in full. What points is he making about society today and throughout the twentieth century?

Using what you have learned from your answers, copy the following table into your books. Then try to complete it by making comparisons and showing how the poems contrast with each other. The first has been started for you.

Regret	*Wilfred Owen shows great regret when he writes about war in 'Dulce Et Decorum Est'. This is shown by...*
Future	
Hope	
Mistakes	
Revulsion	
Curiosity	
Terror	
Sadness	
Lesson	
Frustration	

Plenary

Now you have read all three of the poems and thought about them, see if you have achieved your Aims by working the following exercises.

- Use a quotation – that is, a phrase or line from each of the poems – to illustrate the different styles.
- The poets also use different styles to create an atmosphere. Find a line that expresses the different atmosphere of each of the poems.

Homework

Referring closely to the three poems you have just read, and what you have learned, prepare a five-minute talk about war. You should bear in mind the following points:

- the poets' attitudes towards war and their different experiences;
- the language the poets use to describe their experiences and the way they achieve atmosphere and feeling in their writing;
- any contemporary news stories that are relevant.

Journeys Glossary

accent - The way in which a language is pronounced, which often betrays the social or geographical origin of the speaker.

alliteration - The use of several words together which all begin with the same consonant lettersound.

antonym - A word that means the opposite of another word. For example, 'hot' is the antonym of 'cold'.

argot - A special vocabulary, like a code, understood by a particular group of people, which other people may find difficult to understand.

association - A connection between the meaning of a single word and another idea.

assonance - Repeated vowel sounds that add to the power of the poem.

atmosphere - The general mood.

ballad - A ballad is a long song or poem that tells a story with a current refrain.

chant - A song which delivers a message by repeating the same words over and over again.

colloquial - Informal words used in everyday conversation. Colloquial speech uses non-standard English.

content - Whatever is contained in something i.e. a painting, book, poem, vessel etc.

context - The context of a word or sentence consists of the words or sentences before and after it.

contrast - If you contrast things, you emphasise the differences between them.

convention - A generally accepted way of behaving or doing something.

definition - A statement explaining the meaning of a word, expression or idea.

dialect - A dialect is a form of a language spoken in a particular geographical area.

dirge - A mournful poem or song for the dead.

draft - The first, uncorrected version of a piece of writing.

effective - Working well and producing the hoped for results.

elicit - To find and bring out of.

empathy - The ability to imagine what it is like to be someone or something else.

folklore - Folklore is the traditional stories and beliefs of the community, often passed through the generations.

form - (When applied to poetry) is the shape or pattern it is written in.

formal - Done in accordance with convention and sometimes ceremony.

free verse - Verse that does not follow a set pattern.

haiku - A form of Japanese poetry in three lines of 5, 7 and 5 syllables respectively.

imagery - The pictures created by words.

irony - When humorous words are said that really mean something else.

jargon - Technical language associated with particular activities or groups of people.

justify - To qualify, or make more believable by statement of fact.

lament - A song or a poem about grief.

legend - An old story which has been handed down from earlier times, whose truth cannot be proven.

literary heritage - Plays, poems and novels that have been passed down through the ages and are held in high regard due to their quality.

loose rhyme - Words that almost appear to rhyme but don't.

metaphor - To describe something or someone as having the qualities of something else; e.g. if someone is very shy, you might say they are a mouse.

metaphysical - Concerned with supernatural or religious ideas - things which cannot be explained scientifically.

metre - (In poetry) is the regular and rhythmic arrangement of words and syllables.

mood - Similar to atmosphere and another way of describing it.

monologue - A long speech by one person during a play or conversation.

motto - A sentence to express a collective emotional feeling.

mystic - Someone who believes in spiritual and supernatural happenings.

mystical - Belief in spiritual truths that are beyond understanding.

myth - A traditional story (often featuring gods or heroes) that embodies popular beliefs, or explains a practice, belief or natural phenomenon.

narrative - A text which retells events, often in chronological sequence.

narrator – Whoever is telling the story.

objective - When someone can think about points of view that are not just their own.

obscure - Something that isn't clear.

ode - A poem written in praise of something or someone.

onomatopoeia - Words that sound like the things they represent. 'Buzz' and 'quack' are examples of onomatopoeia.

pace - The speed with which something happens.

paragraph - A section of a piece of writing where a new idea is started , developed and ended. A new paragraph should mark a new topic or a change of focus. In dialogue, a new paragraph marks a change of speaker.

pathos - The quality or power of arousing feelings of pity or sorrow.

penultimate - Next to the last, i.e. paragraph, word etc.

personification - A way of writing whereby things or ideas are made into persons and given a personality.

perspective - An individual way of looking at something.

philosophy - The study or creation of theories about the nature of knowledge and existence.

poetic diction - Specialized language used only in poetry, as the words and figures used would not usually be employed in common speech or prose.

poetic licence - Justifiable departure from conventional rules of grammar, factual accuracy etc for the purpose of creating a desired effect in poetry.

point of view - The way the person telling a story sees the event.

process - The preparing of work.

product - The finished work.

pronoun - A word used instead of repeating the names of who is being discussed.

prose - The form of written language that is not organised according to the formal patterns of verse - i.e. ordinary written language.

pseudonym - A name a writer uses to cover up who they are.

qualify - If you qualify a statement, you add detail or explanation to change it slightly.

quatrain - A stanza of four lines.

rap - A style of poetry that has a strong rhythmic beat as the words are spoken (often a fast monologue set to music).

re-drafting – Improving work by making changes to it.

re-draft - The correcting of work after the first draft.

reflect - To consider carefully

refrain - A phrase or line of a poem, repeated at intervals, sometimes in each stanza.

repetition - Words or parts of words that are repeated throughout a piece of writing.

retort - A short, angry reply.

review - Examine a piece of writing carefully looking at all its various features, i.e. power of language, ability to interest, capacity to cover what it sets out to say etc.

rhyme scheme - The pattern in which the rhymed line-endings are arranged in a poem or in a stanza.

rhyming couplet - Two lines of poetry forming a pair with a rhyming word at the end of each line.

rhythm - (In poetry) the regular movement or beat formed by the pattern of stressed and unstressed syllables in the words.

Romantic era - A literary movement in the late eighteenth and early nineteenth centuries during which writers concentrated on feelings and the imagination as opposed to rational scientific ideas.

scan - Read to search for specific words or points.

sensory - Concerned with sensations or the senses.

sestet - Six lines that follow each other.

sestina - A verse form in which the six final words of the lines in the first stanza are repeated in a different order in each of the remaining five stanzas.

simile - The comparing of one thing to another by using the word 'as' or 'like'.

skim - Read through quickly to find out what the writer is saying.

sonnet - A poem of 14 lines, usually expressing a single idea or sentiment.

standard English - The type of spoken and written English that should be used when formal language is appropriate. Standard English is the language spoken and written by the majority of educated speakers of English and is taught in schools.

stanza - Several lines of verse grouped together.

stream of consciousness - A continuous flow of ideas, thoughts, feelings and memories from the human mind, often in an unpunctuated, disjointed form.

subjective - Influenced by personal feelings and opinion rather than based on fact or rational thought.

style - The way in which something is done or presented. Somebody's writing style is the individual way in which they use language.

subject - Whatever a thing is about.

syllable - A part of a word containing a single vowel-like sound which is pronounced as a unit. For example, 'book' has one syllable and 'reading' has two.

symbol - Something that represents or stands for something else, with which it is associated.

synonym - A word that has a very similar meaning to another word. e.g. 'clap' and 'applaud' can mean almost the same thing.

theme - A main idea, topic or issue which is expressed or developed in writing. It can also apply to painting, film or music.

tone - The tone of a piece of writing is its style and the ideas and opinions expressed in it, i.e. playful, sombre etc.

traditional - Based on customs and handed down through the ages.

villanelle - A poem in a fixed form of 19 lines, arranged in six stanzas. The first five stanzas have three lines each, and the last has four. The first and third line of the first stanza are repeated alternately as last lines from the second to fifth and end in the sixth.

wordplay - The making of jokes through clever use of words.